John Connor Press Associates

About the Author

MITCHELL SYMONS, author of *This Book . . . of More Perfectly Useless Information* and *Why Girls Can't Throw . . . and Other Questions You Always Wanted Answered*, was born in London and educated at the London School of Economics (the alma mater of JFK and Mick Jagger), where he studied law. Since leaving BBC TV, where he was a researcher and then a director, he has worked as a writer, broadcaster, and journalist. He lives on the southern coast of England with his wife and sons and any number of their pet animals.

That Book

Also by Mitchell Symons

Nonfiction

*Why Girls Can't Throw . . . and Other Questions
You Always Wanted Answered*

The Other Book . . . of the Most Perfectly Useless Information

This Book . . . of More Perfectly Useless Information

Forfeit!

The Equation Book of Sports Crosswords

The Equation Book of Movie Crosswords

The You Magazine Book of Journalists (four books; coauthor)

Movielists (coauthor)

The Sunday Magazine Book of Crosswords

The Hello! Magazine Book of Crosswords (three books)

How to Be Fat: The Chip and Fry Diet (coauthor)

The Book of Criminal Records

The Book of Lists

The Book of Celebrity Lists

The Book of Celebrity Sex Lists

The Bill Clinton Joke Book

The National Lottery Big Draw 2000 (coauthor)

Fiction

All In

The Lot

That Book

...OF PERFECTLY USELESS INFORMATION

Mitchell Symons

HARPER

NEW YORK • LONDON • TORONTO • SYDNEY

HARPER

This book was originally published in the UK by Transworld Publishers in
2003. It is hereby reprinted by arrangement with Transworld Publishers.

A hardcover edition of this book was published in the U.S. in 2004 by
HarperEntertainment, an imprint of HarperCollins Publishers.

HarperCollins books may be purchased for educational, business, or
sales promotional use. For information please write: Special Markets
Department, HarperCollins Publishers, 10 East 53rd Street,
New York, NY 10022.

First Harper paperback published 2006.

Designed by Chris Welch

The Library of Congress has catalogued the hardcover edition as follows:

Symons, Mitchell.
    That book: . . . of perfectly useless information / by Mitchell Symons.—
1st ed.
        p. cm.
    Includes index.
    ISBN 0-06-073149-4
        1. Handbooks, vade-mecums, etc. I. Title.
AG106.S94 2004
031.02—dc22   2004048111

ISBN-10: 0-06-073254-7 (pbk.)
ISBN-13: 978-0-06-073254-7 (pbk.)

06 07 08 09 10 DIX/RRD 10 9 8 7 6 5 4 3 2 1

To my darling wife, Penny, and to our wonderful sons, Jack and Charlie

There is much pleasure to be gained from
useless knowledge.

—BERTRAND RUSSELL

That
Book

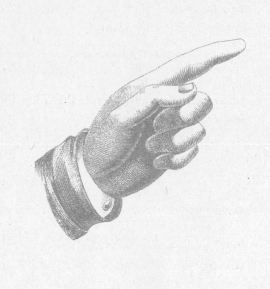

Fathers

Uma Thurman's father was the first American to be ordained a Buddhist monk.

Stephen King's father went out for a pack of cigarettes and never returned.

Julianna Margulies's father wrote the "Plop, Plop, Fizz, Fizz" jingle for Alka-Seltzer.

Laura Dern was bullied at school because her father—Bruce Dern—was "the only person to kill John Wayne in the movies."

Rachel Weisz's father invented the artificial respirator.

Bob Marley had a white Liverpudlian father.

Elvis Costello's father sang the "I'm a Secret Lemonade Drinker" jingle for R. White's lemonade.

Eminem, Eartha Kitt, Lance Armstrong, Charlie Chaplin, Bill Clinton, Evander Holyfield (whose father had twenty-seven children), Vanilla Ice, Eric Clapton, Rod Steiger, Lee Trevino, Naomi Campbell and Mike Tyson never knew their fathers.

The fathers of George Michael and Yusuf Islam (Cat Stevens) were both Greek restaurateurs.

Stockard Channing received a substantial inheritance at the age of fifteen after the death of her shipping-magnate father.

Ben Affleck's reformed-alcoholic father, Tim, became Robert Downey Jr.'s drug counselor.

The fathers of Roger Moore, Burt Reynolds, Queen Latifah, Arnold Schwarzenegger and Eddie Murphy were all policemen.

The fathers of Otis Redding, Jane Austen, David Frost, Alice Cooper, John Hurt, Ike Turner, Denzel Washington, Rita Coolidge, Aretha Franklin, Laurence Olivier, Tori Amos, Nina Simone, Pearl Bailey, Ingmar Berman, Alistair Cooke, George McGovern, Walter Mondale, Agnes Moorehead, Dean Rusk, Frances McDormand and Jessica Simpson were all clergymen.

The fathers of Harry Houdini, Erich Segal, Jackie Mason and Isaac Asimov were all rabbis.

The fathers of Gil Scott-Heron, Ian McShane and Colin Farrell were all professional soccer players.

The fathers of Glenn Close, Pamela Stephenson, Katharine Hepburn, Jacqueline Bisset, Brian De Palma, Jane Seymour, Bill Pullman, Edvard Munch, Willem Dafoe, Kate Bush, Judi Dench, Tom Stoppard, Humphrey Bogart, Ben Kingsley, Hillary Clinton, Lisa Kudrow, Reese Witherspoon and Gavin Rossdale were all doctors.

Emilio Estevez (Martin Sheen), Jennifer Jason Leigh (Vic Morrow) and Norah Jones (Ravi Shankar) all have/had famous fathers but found fame themselves with different surnames.

People whose fathers died in World War I: Barbara Cartland, David Niven, Ninette de Valois, Albert Camus.

People whose fathers died in World War II: John Phillips, John Ehrlichman, the Duke of Kent, Gerhard Schroeder, Roger Waters

The fathers of Ricky Gervais, Julie Walters, Glenda Jackson, Bill Wyman and Boy George all worked in the building trade.

The fathers of Jim Carrey and Jeremy Irons were both accountants.

The fathers of Jerry Hall and Sean Connery were both truck drivers.

The fathers of Faye Dunaway and Christina Aguilera were both U.S. Army sergeants.

The fathers of Rupert Everett and Elizabeth Hurley were both British army majors.

The fathers of Mick Jagger and Ewan McGregor were both PE teachers.

The fathers of Robert Redford, Sting and Emma Bunton (Baby Spice) were all milkmen.

The fathers of Russell Crowe and Patricia Hodge were both hoteliers.

Olivia Newton-John's father was a headmaster.

The fathers of Robert Duvall and Jim Morrison were admirals in the U.S. Navy, while Kris Kristofferson's father was a U.S. Air Force general.

Rufus Sewell's father was an animator who worked on *Yellow Submarine*.

Anthony Quinn (81), Charlie Chaplin (73), Clint Eastwood (66), Cary Grant (62), Yves Montand (67), Marlon Brando (65), Pablo Picasso (68), Francisco de Goya (68), Saul Bellow (84), James Doohan (80) and James Brown (67) all became fathers past the age of 60.

Sylvia Plath, Charlotte Brontë and Gloria Vanderbilt all had father fixations.

The fathers of Judy Garland, Jacqueline Onassis, Liza Minnelli and Anne Heche were all gay.

The fathers of Michael Redgrave and Jeffrey Archer were both bigamists.

"**To be** a successful father, there's one absolute rule: when you have a kid, don't look at it for the first two years." (Ernest Hemingway)

"**Fathers should** neither be seen nor heard. That is the only proper basis for family life." (Oscar Wilde)

"**The most** important thing a father can do for his children is to love their mother." (Theodore Hesburgh)

"**The fundamental** defect of fathers is that they want their children to be a credit to them." (Bertrand Russell)

"**My father** told me all about the birds and the bees. The liar—I went steady with a woodpecker till I was twenty-one." (Bob Hope)

"**It's a** wonderful feeling when your father becomes not a god but a whole man. When he comes down from the mountain and you see this man with weaknesses. And you love him as this whole being—not just a figurehead." (Robin Williams)

"**When I** was a boy of fourteen, my father was so ignorant I could hardly stand to have the old man around. But when I got to twenty-one, I was astonished at how much he had learned in seven years." (Mark Twain)

"**My dad** was always there for me, and I want my kids to have the same." (Kevin Costner)

"**My dad** is a lot smarter than I am, and his line of integrity is to a fault." (George Clooney)

"My father was frightened of his mother. I was frightened of my father, and I'm damned well going to make sure that my children are frightened of me." (King George V)

"I looked up to my father too much to really open my heart to him. We were almost formal. I did not tell him I loved him. All I can do is hope that he would have known." (Hugh Laurie)

Mothers

Eric Clapton, Jack Nicholson and Bobby Darin had mothers who the rest of the world thought were their sisters; indeed, Darin was thirty-two before he discovered that his "mother" was actually his grandmother and that his "sister" was his mother.

Charlton Heston's mother's maiden name was Charlton.

When Michael Caine was a child, his mother pasted his ears to his head to stop them from sticking out.

Victoria Principal's mother's maiden name was Ree Veal.

David Schwimmer's mother is the attorney who handled Roseanne's first divorce.

Telly Savalas and Tommy Lee both had mothers who won the Miss Greece beauty contest.

Shirley MacLaine (Beaty), Marilyn Monroe (Baker), Lauren Bacall (Perske), Catherine Deneuve (Dorléac), Kevin Spacey (Fowler), Beck Hansen (Campbell), Chris De Burgh (Davidson), Elvis Costello (MacManus), Ian Holm (Cuthbert) all used their mother's maiden name instead of their father's surname.

Priscilla Presley and Claudia Cardinale both became mothers again after becoming grandmothers.

Uma Thurman's mother had been married to Timothy Leary before marrying Uma's father.

Shirley Williams (Vera Brittain), Liza Minnelli (Judy Garland), Joely Richardson (Vanessa Redgrave), Mia Farrow (Maureen O'Sullivan), Jennifer Ehle (Rosemary Harris), Carrie Fisher (Debbie Reynolds), Melanie Griffith (Tippi Hedren) and Kate Hudson (Goldie Hawn) all have/had famous mothers but found fame themselves with different surnames.

James Cagney, Adolf Hitler, D. H. Lawrence, Marcel Proust, Liberace, Gustav Mahler, J. M. Barrie, Sigmund Freud, Elvis Presley, Peter Tchaikovsky, Harry Houdini, Frank Lloyd Wright and Isaac Newton all had mother fixations.

The mothers of Oscar Wilde, Peter O'Toole, Ernest Hemingway, General Douglas MacArthur, Bill Tilden and Franklin D. Roosevelt dressed their sons as girls for the first few years of their lives.

The mothers of Sarah Bernhardt and Clara Bow were both prostitutes.

The mothers of Patrick Macnee and Jodie Foster were both lesbians.

"My mother was an incredible character who was very funny and would outride any storm." (Michael Caine)

"My mother was consumed with her own interest, which was gambling. She was really very self-centered." (Michael Winner)

"I look so much like my mum, especially when I dress up as a woman." (Terry Jones)

"The mother is the one who tells you you are beautiful. The mother is the one who keeps reassuring you during those times of insecurity, who keeps your chin up. And I didn't have that." (Mick Hucknall, whose mother left when he was three)

"My mother is a wonderful, eccentric lady who has no concept whatever of interior monologue. We'll be driving along in the car and she'll suddenly say, 'Ants don't like cucumbers, you know. And roaches don't like cinnamon. Do you want some cheese, Michael? Rembrandt was the Lord of the day.' " (Mike Myers)

"My mother's death was the most painful thing, because I was so close to her. When you lose someone dear, it really encourages you to seize every day, you know, because no one knows how long they've got." (Ronan Keating)

"There are only two things a child will share willingly—communicable diseases and his mother's age." (Benjamin Spock)

"My mother loved children—she would have given anything if I had been one." (Groucho Marx)

"I modeled Tootsie on my mother, who was a great character. Sadly she didn't live to see it as she died while I was making the movie, but she's in it." (Dustin Hoffman)

"When I told my mother I was going to marry a Catholic, she couldn't hear me because her head was in the oven." (Mel Brooks)

"My mum was a great feminist and always said, 'Hold your head high—no matter what happens. It's fine, as long as you know you've conducted yourself properly.' " (Nicole Kidman)

"My mother gave me two pieces of advice: 'Never talk about the movies you didn't do and never talk specifically about men.' " (Gwyneth Paltrow)

"My mother's best advice to me was: 'To thine own self be true.' She often thought Polonius was much maligned. She is the smartest woman I know, with a mind like a steel trap." (Ben Affleck)

"My mom's a tough bird and one of my best friends in the world. She told me when I was very young, 'Don't ever take any crap off anybody, ever.' All through my teens and to this day, I don't." (Johnny Depp)

"There's nothing I won't tell my mother. Nothing. We talk every day on the telephone." (Claudia Schiffer)

"When I was growing up, the biggest influence in my life was my mother. She made great sacrifices to send me to private school, and I will always be grateful for that." (Naomi Campbell)

Words

Stewardesses is the longest word that is typed with only the left hand.

The only 15-letter word that can be spelled without repeating a letter is *uncopyrightable*.

Shakespeare invented more than 1,700 words (including *assassination* and *bump*).

If you mouth the word *colorful* to someone, it looks like you are saying, "I love you"

There is no Albanian word for *headache*.

Just 1,000 words make up 90 percent of all writing.

No word in the English language rhymes with *orange*, *silver* or *month*.

The Hawaiian alphabet has only 12 letters.

Dreamt is the only English word that ends in the letters *mt*.

Queue is the only word in the English language to be pronounced the same way even if the last four letters are removed.

Zenith, tariff, *sherbet, algebra, carafe, syrup, cotton, mattress* and *alcohol* are all derived from Arabic.

The following words are rarely used in the singular: *trivia (trivium), paparazzi (paparazzo), assizes (assize), auspices (auspice), timpani (timpano), minutiae (minutia), grafitti (grafitto), scampi (scampo), scruples (scruple), measles (measle).*

The following words are rarely used in the positive: *advertent, maculate, clement, consolate, delible, feckful, furl, sipid, speakable, kempt, corrigible, placable, effable, nocuous, pervious, expurgated, peccable, evitable.*

The expression *rule of thumb* derives from the old English law that said you couldn't beat your wife with anything wider than your thumb.

The name *jeep* came from the abbreviation GP, used in the U.S. Army for general-purpose vehicle.

The word *chunder* comes from convict ships bound for Australia: when people were going to vomit, they used to shout, "Watch under!"

The word *bigwig* takes its name from King Louis IV of France, who used to wear big wigs.

There are only two words in the English language ending in -*gry*: hungry and angry.

The longest one-syllable word is *screeched.*

Skepticism **is** the longest word that alternates hands when you're typing.

The word *dude* was coined by Oscar Wilde and his friends. It is a combination of the words *duds* and *attitude.*

Hijinks **is** the only word with three dotted letters in a row.

Tom Cruise, Cher, Henry Winkler, Sarah Miles, Jackie Stewart, Walt Disney, Whoopi Goldberg, Thomas Edison, Leonardo da Vinci, Richard Branson, Noel Gallagher, Guy Ritchie, Tommy Hilfiger, Liv Tyler, Robbie Williams and Ozzy Osbourne have all suffered from dyslexia.

Gerard Depardieu, Bill Clinton, Bill Gates, Hu Jintao, Simon Wiesenthal, Wolfgang Mozart, Robert Mitchum, Truman Capote, Mr. T and Chico Marx all have had photographic memories.

The Names of Things You Didn't Know Had Names

Rowel: the revolving star on the back of a cowboy's spurs

Columella: the bottom part of the nose that separates the nostrils

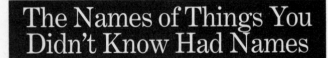

Saddle: the rounded part on the top of a book of matches

Ophyron: the space between your eyebrows

Rasceta: the creases on the inside of your wrist

Purlicue: the space between the extended thumb and index finger

Nittles: the punctuation marks designed to denote swear words in comics

Ferrule: the metal band on the top of a pencil that holds the eraser in place

Peen: on a hammer, the end opposite the striking face

Obdormition: when an arm or a leg "goes to sleep" as a result of numbness caused by pressure on a nerve

Keeper: the loop on a belt that holds the end in place after it has passed through the buckle

Armsate: the hole in a shirt or a sweater through which you put your hand and arm

Things That Are Not What They Seem

Rice paper contains not a grain of rice.

French fries originated in Belgium, not France.

Great Danes come from Germany, not Denmark.

Ten-gallon hats hold only about 6 pints of water.

Koala bears aren't bears, they're marsupials.

Mountain goats aren't goats, they're small antelopes.

Fireflies aren't flies, they're beetles.

The funny bone isn't a bone, it's a nerve.

Jackrabbits aren't rabbits, they're hares.

Shooting stars are meteors.

Prairie dogs aren't dogs, they're rodents.

Guinea pigs aren't pigs, nor are they from Guinea: they're South American rodents.

Catgut isn't made from cats, it's made from sheep.

Lead pencils contain no lead, only graphite.

Glowworms aren't worms, they're beetles.

The horned toad isn't a toad, it's a lizard.

Bombay duck isn't duck, it's dried fish.

Turkish baths originated in ancient Rome, not in Turkey.

Silkworms aren't worms, they're caterpillars.

Peanuts aren't nuts, they're legumes.

Spoonerisms

"Kinquering congs their titles take."

"Let us drink to the queer old dean."

"The Lord is a shoving leopard."

"That is just a half-warmed fish."

"The cat popped on its drawers."

"Is the bean dizzy?"

"Please sew me to another sheet."

"You will leave by the next town drain."

The Human Condition

Only 1 person in 2 billion will live to be 116 or older.

The human body grows the equivalent of a new skeleton every 7 years.

A newborn baby's heart beats twice as fast as an adult's.

The average person's heart beats 36 million times a year.

Adult humans have 206 bones. At birth, an infant has 350 bones. As the child grows, many bones fuse with other bones.

A quarter of the 206 bones in the human body are in the feet.

As a child grows, the body part that grows least is the eye. While the rest of an adult body is 20 times bigger than it was at birth, the eye is only three and a quarter times bigger.

Women get more migraines than men do.

The average person is a quarter of an inch taller at night.

Fingernails grow 4 times faster than toenails.

The average person sleeps for about 220,000 hours (or just over 25 years) in a lifetime.

Humans are the only animals that cry emotional tears.

It takes just 1 minute for blood to travel through the whole human body.

People who live in the city have longer, thicker nose hairs than people who live in the country.

The first of the 5 senses to go with age is smell.

More boys than girls are born during the day; more girls are born at night.

Your stomach has to produce a new layer of mucus every 2 weeks; otherwise it will digest itself.

The human sneeze travels at 600 miles per hour.

The strongest muscle in the body is the tongue.

You can't kill yourself by holding your breath.

Right-handed people live, on average, 9 years longer than left-handed people do.

Humans are the only primates that don't have pigment in the palms of their hands.

Men get more ulcers than women do.

Children have more taste buds than adults do.

Your tongue print is as unique as your fingerprints.

If you yelled for 8 years, 7 months and 6 days, you would have produced enough sound energy to heat 1 cup of coffee.

The human heart creates enough pressure while pumping to squirt blood 30 feet.

Banging your head against a wall uses 150 calories an hour.

We shed an average of 40 pounds of dead skin in a lifetime.

The average person laughs 15 times a day.

Pain travels through our bodies at a speed of 350 feet a second.

When we blush, our stomach lining also turns red.

Our eyes don't freeze in very cold weather because of the salt in our tears.

Women blink nearly twice as often as men do.

We get goose bumps where our ancestors used to have hair.

Humans are the only animals to sleep on their backs.

The brain weighs three pounds but uses some 20 percent of the body's blood and oxygen.

The average person has 100,000 hairs on his or her head—but redheads have fewer and blonds have more.

On a square inch of our skin, there are 20 million microscopic animals.

The average human eats 8 spiders in his or her lifetime at night.

Babies are born without kneecaps. They don't appear until the child reaches 2 to 6 years of age.

If you farted continuously for 6 years and 9 months, enough wind would be produced to equal the energy of an atomic bomb.

Science

The microwave was invented after a researcher walked by a radar tube and a chocolate bar melted in his pocket.

Grapes explode when you put them in the microwave.

There are more than 1,000 chemicals in a cup of coffee; of these, only 26 have been tested, and half of them caused cancer in rats.

A rainbow can occur only when the sun is 40 degrees or less above the horizon.

Cut an onion in half, rub it on the sole of your foot, and an hour later you'll taste onion in your mouth.

In 10 minutes a hurricane releases more energy than all the world's nuclear weapons combined.

Britney Spears, Anna Kournikova, Osama bin Laden, Avril Lavigne, Michelangelo and Tonya Harding have all had computer viruses named after them.

Around the World

Disney World is bigger than the world's 5 smallest countries.

The Danish flag—dating back to the thirteenth century—is the world's oldest unchanged national flag.

Italy's national flag was designed by Napoleon.

There is a city called Rome in every continent.

There are 3 American towns named Santa Claus.

Istanbul is the only city in the world to be in 2 continents (Europe and Asia).

Los Angeles's full name is "El Pueblo de Nuestra Señora la Reina de los Angeles de Porciuncula" and can be abbreviated to 3.63 percent of its size: "L.A."

Americans on average eat 18 acres of pizza every day.

All the continents are wider in the north than in the south.

You could drive a car around the world 4 times with the amount of fuel in a jumbo jet

If the population of China walked past you in single file, the line would never end because of the rate of reproduction.

China has more English speakers than the United States does.

Mongolians put salt in their tea instead of sugar.

Antarctica is the only continent without snakes or reptiles.

Ten percent of the Russian government's income comes from the sale of vodka.

The glue on Israeli postage stamps is certified kosher.

The highest point in Pennsylvania is lower than the lowest point in Colorado.

The Dead Sea is really a lake.

Q is the only letter that doesn't appear in the names of any of the fifty states of the U.S.

There isn't a (real) river in the whole of Saudi Arabia.

If all the Antarctic ice melted, the ocean level would rise nearly 250 feet, and 25 percent of the world's land surface would be flooded.

Essential Facts

There are 293 ways to make change for a dollar.

Nutmeg is extremely poisonous if injected intravenously.

111,111,111 x 111, 111, 111 = 12,345,678,987,654,321.

Pearls melt in vinegar.

No former American president has ever died in the month of May.

If pack-a-day smokers inhaled a week's worth of nicotine, they would die instantly.

Volleyball is the most popular sport at nudist camps.

The buttons on a man's jacket cuff were originally intended to stop manservants from wiping their noses on the sleeves of their uniforms.

Watching TV uses up 50 percent more calories than sleeping does.

Twenty percent of the people in the whole history of mankind who have lived beyond the age of 65 are alive today.

On average, a drop of Heinz tomato ketchup leaves the bottle at a speed of 25 miles per year.

At any given moment, there are some 1,800 thunderstorms somewhere on the planet Earth.

Tuesday Weld was born on a Friday.

Six out of 7 gynecologists are men.

The Bible is the most shoplifted book in the United States.

Strawberries have more vitamin C than oranges do.

Pollen lasts forever.

If Barbie—whose full name is Barbara Millicent Roberts—were life size, her measurements would be 39-23-33, she would stand 7 feet, 2 inches tall, and she would have a neck twice the length of a normal human's neck.

No piece of paper can be folded in half more than 7 times.

Animals

Besides humans, the only animal that can stand on its head is the elephant.

There isn't a single reference to a cat in the Bible.

Nearly all polar bears are left-handed.

A newborn panda is smaller than a mouse.

The heads of a freak two-headed snake will fight over food—despite sharing the same stomach.

The armadillo is the only animal—apart from man—that can catch leprosy.

The elephant is the only animal with 4 knees.

Some snakes can live up to a year without eating.

A beaver can chop down more than 200 trees in a year.

Besides humans, the only animals that can suffer sunburn are pigs and horses.

Giraffes can live without water for longer than camels can.

The average rabbit takes 18 naps a day.

The basenji is the only dog that doesn't bark.

A pig's orgasm lasts for 30 minutes.

It takes a male horse only 14 seconds to copulate.

The elephant is the only mammal that can't jump.

A skunk will not bite and throw its scent at the same time.

Cats have over 100 vocal sounds; dogs have only about 10.

The female nutria, a furry rodent, is the only mammal with nipples along its backbone.

A donkey will sink in quicksand, but a mule won't.

Pigs can become alcoholics.

Tigers have striped skin, not just striped fur.

The reindeer is the only female animal with antlers.

Polar bears can smell a human being from 20 miles away.

Most dinosaurs were no bigger than chickens.

When hippopotamuses get upset, their sweat turns red.

Of all the mammal species in the world, almost a quarter are bats.

No new animals have been domesticated in the last 4,000 years.

The world's biggest frog is bigger than the world's smallest antelope.

An angry gorilla pokes its tongue out.

A dog can't hear the lowest key on a piano.

The normal temperature of a cat is 101.5 degrees.

A giraffe can clean its ears with its tongue.

Snakes hear through their jaws.

Camel milk does not curdle.

The stomach of a hippopotamus is 10 feet long.

A rat can last longer without water than a camel can.

Kangaroos can't walk backward.

Cats can't taste sweet food.

Gorillas can't swim.

There are more goats than people in Somalia.

Deer sleep only 5 minutes a day.

Insects, Etc.

A male spider's reproductive organ is located at the end of one of his legs.

The average caterpillar has 2,000 muscles in its body (we humans have 656).

Tarantulas can go for up to 2 years without eating.

Anteaters can stick out their tongues up to 160 times a minute.

Mother tarantulas kill 99 percent of the babies they hatch.

Queen bees only ever use their stingers to kill other queen bees.

Queen termites can live for up to 100 years.

The only food cockroaches won't eat is cucumbers.

There are more insects in a square mile of rural land than there are human beings on the entire earth.

Flies take off backward.

A moth has no stomach.

Mosquitoes are attracted to people who have recently eaten bananas.

A greenfly born on Sunday can be a grandparent by Wednesday.

The silkworm has 11 brains. But it uses only 5 of them.

A leech can drink up to 8 times its weight in blood at one sitting.

The housefly hums in the middle-octave key of F.

The flea can jump 350 times its body length.

A cockroach can live for several weeks after being decapitated.

The snail has retractable antennae.

Gram for gram, a bumblebee is 150 times stronger than an elephant.

An ant can survive for 2 weeks underwater.

The male gypsy moth can "smell" the virgin female gypsy moth from a distance of 1.8 miles.

Snails can sleep for 3 years without eating.

The ant can lift 50 times its own weight and can pull 30 times its own weight.

The praying mantis is the only insect that can turn its head without moving its body.

A bee is more likely to sting you on a windy day.

Fish, Etc.

Starfish don't have brains.

The catfish has over 27,000 taste buds (more than any other creature on the planet).

Goldfish kept in a darkened room eventually turn white.

The baby blue whale gains 10 pounds in weight per hour.

Whale songs rhyme.

The male rather than the female seahorse carries the eggs.

The starfish is the only creature on the planet that can turn its stomach inside out.

A goldfish has a memory span of 3 seconds.

The giant squid has the largest eyes in the world.

A pregnant goldfish is called a "twit."

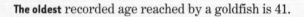

The oldest recorded age reached by a goldfish is 41.

The white shark is the only sea creature with no natural enemies

Dolphins sleep with one eye open.

A blue whale's tongue weighs more than an elephant.

Nine out of every 10 living things live in the ocean.

Fish don't have eyelids.

A shark is the only fish that can blink with both eyes.

The heart of a blue whale is the size of a small car.

If a mackerel or a shark stops swimming, it dies.

Squids can commit suicide by eating their own tentacles.

The female starfish produces 2 million eggs a year, of which 99 percent are eaten by other fish.

Walruses are almost always right-handed.

An octopus has 3 hearts.

History

Each king in a deck of playing cards represents a great king from history: spades—King David; clubs—Alexander the Great; hearts—Charlemagne; diamonds—Julius Caesar.

The only painting Vincent van Gogh sold in his lifetime was *The Red Vineyard*.

The Roman emperor Nero "married" his male slave Scotus.

Michelangelo's cook was illiterate, so he drew her a shopping list— which today is priceless.

Spiral staircases in medieval castles ran clockwise so that attacking knights climbing the stairs couldn't use their right hands—their sword hands—while the defending knights coming down could. And left-handed men, believed to descend from the devil, couldn't become knights.

The shortest war in history was between Zanzibar and England in 1896: Zanzibar surrendered after thirty-eight minutes.

February 1865 is the only month in recorded history not to have a full moon.

Pirates wore earrings in the belief that it improved their eyesight.

The architect who built the Kremlin had his eyes gouged out by Ivan the Terrible so that he'd never be able to design another building like it.

In ancient Egypt, priests plucked every hair from their bodies, including their eyebrows and eyelashes.

U.S. presidents John F. Kennedy and Warren Harding were both survived by their fathers.

Adolf Hitler's mother seriously considered having an abortion but was talked out of it by her doctor.

Cleopatra wrote a book on cosmetics. One of the ingredients was burned mice.

All seventeen children of Queen Anne died before she did.

The first country to abolish capital punishment was Austria, in 1787.

Richard the Lionheart spent just four months of his life in England.

The Wright brothers' first flight was shorter than the wingspan of a 747.

Lady Macbeth had a son called Lulach the Fatuous.

Mexico once had three presidents in a single day.

Leonardo da Vinci could write with one hand and draw with the other at the same time.

Birds, Etc.

The longest recorded flight of a chicken is 13 seconds.

Female canaries can't sing.

The ptarmigan turns completely white in the winter.

The average ostrich's eye is the size of a tennis ball and bigger than its brain.

There is the same number of chickens in the world as humans.

The waste produced by a single chicken in its lifetime could supply enough electricity to run a 100-watt bulb for 5 hours.

The most common bird in the world is the starling.

The hummingbird is the only bird that can fly backward.

The average life span of a parrot is 120 years.

The golden eagle can spot a rabbit from nearly 2 miles away.

The penguin is the only bird that walks upright (it is also the only bird that can swim but not fly).

Flamingos can eat only with their heads upside down.

Bats always turn left when leaving a cave.

Ostriches yawn in groups before going to sleep.

Owls (not even bluebirds) are the only birds that can see the color blue.

Pigeons are the only birds that can drink water without having to raise their heads to swallow.

Bluebirds can't see the color blue.

Condors can fly 10 miles without flapping their wings.

The bones of a pigeon weigh less than its feathers.

Unlike humans, canaries can regenerate their brain cells.

The chaffinch cannot sing anything original; it can only imitate the songs of other birds.

Seventy-five percent of wild birds die before they are 6 months old.

A woodpecker can peck 20 times a second.

Things That Started in the 1950s

Rock 'n' roll, nuclear submarines, credit cards, NATO, the Miss World contest, *This Is Your Life*, tea bags, the Frisbee, tranquilizers, Disneyland, *The Guinness Book of Records*, space travel, Lego, transistor hearing aids, Cinemascope, diet soft drinks (no-cal ginger ale), the Yellow Pages, Barbie dolls, automatic electric kettles, heart pacemakers, typewriter correction fluid, microwave ovens, Velcro, nonstick saucepans, the Moonies, polio vaccines, Beatniks, kidney transplants, roll-on deodorants, boutiques, disposable diapers

The Odds Against Various Eventualities

Being struck by lightning: 1 in 10 million

Being killed by a bee sting: 1 in 6 million

Giving birth to quintuplets: 1 in 57 million births—without fertility treatment

Hitting two holes-in-one during the same round of golf: 1 in 8 million

Becoming an alcoholic if you drink regularly: 1 in 10

Being hijacked on a plane by terrorists twice in the same year: 1 in 150 million

Being hit by a meteorite: 1 in 200 million

A woman's being color-blind: 1 in 1,000 (women are ten times less likely than men to suffer from color blindness)

An adult's catching head lice in any given year: 1 in 100

Dying in an airplane crash: 1 in 2.2 million

A male's being impotent between the ages of twenty and thirty: 1 in 124

Choking to death on food: 1 in 250,000

Getting killed in a road accident: 1 in 15,800

Going into a permanent vegetative state following a head injury: 1 in 1 million

Getting kidney stones in any year: 1 in 100

Your as-yet unborn child's growing up to be a stutterer: 1 in 400

Flying on an airplane with the same flight number as a plane that crashed: 0 (flight numbers are always eliminated after a crash)

Maniacs

Kleptomaniac (person obsessed with stealing)

Chionomaniac (snow)

Ablutomaniac (bathing)

Timbromaniac (stamps)

Pyromaniac (fire)

Nudomaniac (nudity)

Cynomaniac (dogs)

Ailuromaniac (cats)

Ichthyomaniac (fish)

Oniomaniac (buying)

Arithomaniac (counting)

Philopatridomaniac (homesickness)

Bruxomaniac (grinding teeth)

Klazomaniac (shouting)

Catapedamaniac (jumping from high places)

Onychotillomaniac (picking nails)

Cresomaniac (personal wealth)

Phagomaniac (food)

Titillomaniac (scratching)

Erythromaniac (blushing)

Dromomaniac (traveling)

Murphy's Law

Anything that can go wrong will go wrong.

The first place to look for something is the last place you would expect to find it.

When someone says, "It's not the money, it's the principle," nine times out of ten, it's the money.

Whenever you make a journey by bicycle, it's always more uphill than downhill.

As soon as you mention some-thing, a) if it's good, it goes away; b) if it's bad, it happens.

You never find something until you replace it.

When the train you are on is late, the bus to take you home from the station will be on time.

If an experiment works, something has gone wrong.

It always rains when you've just washed your car, but washing your car to make it rain won't work.

When you dial a wrong number, it's never busy.

Checks get lost in the mail, but bills never do.

In a supermarket the other lines always move faster than yours.

Illnesses always start on a Friday evening . . . but end on a Monday morning.

Friends come and go, but enemies accumulate.

The odds of the bread's falling butter-side-down are directly proportional to the value of the carpet.

The severity of an itch is inversely proportional to how easy it is to scratch.

If during a month only three enjoyable social activities take place, they will all happen on the same evening.

The only way to get a bank loan is to prove you don't need one.

Singular People

Samuel L. Jackson was Bill Cosby's stand-in for three years on *The Cosby Show*.

Chuck Berry invented his duck walk initially to hide the creases in his suit.

John Wayne once won the dog Lassie from its owner in a poker game.

Jack Nicholson was in detention every day for a whole school year.

Olivia Newton-John is president of the Isle of Man Basking Sharks Society

Mariah Carey's vocal range spans five octaves.

Nick Nolte ate real dog food in the film *Down and Out in Beverly Hills* (when he was showing the dog how to eat from a dog bowl).

Florence Nightingale used to travel everywhere with a pet owl in her pocket.

Melissa Joan Hart can recite the mathematical expression pi to 400 decimal places.

Nicolas Cage ate a live cockroach for *Vampire's Kiss*.

Winston Churchill smoked an estimated 300,000 cigars in his lifetime.

Tom Cruise has saved three lives—in Santa Monica, off the island of Capri and in London.

Ben Stiller was taught how to swim by the Pips (as in Gladys Knight & the Pips).

Amanda Peet can recite all the lines from *Tootsie* and *A Chorus Line*.

Richard Gere never swears. If visitors swear in his home, he asks them to leave.

Pierce Brosnan bought the typewriter of James Bond creator Ian Fleming for approximately $80,000.

When he was a teenager, Colin Farrell put Smarties under his pillow to bring Marilyn Monroe back from the dead.

Isaac Asimov is the only author to have a book in every Dewey-decimal category.

All the Golden Raspberry Awards (or Razzies) for Worst Film, Worst Actor and Worst Actress

For 2004 (awarded in 2005): *Catwoman;* George W. Bush (*Fahrenheit 9/11*); Halle Berry (*Catwoman*)

For 2003 (awarded in 2004): *Gigli;* Ben Affleck (*Gigli*); Jennifer Lopez (*Gigli*)

For 2002 (awarded in 2003): *Swept Away;* Roberto Benigni (*Pinocchio*); Madonna (*Swept Away*) tied with Britney Spears (*Crossroads*)

For 2001: *Freddy Got Fingered;* Tom Green (*Freddy Got Fingered*); Mariah Carey (*Glitter*)

For 2000: *Battlefield Earth;* John Travolta (*Battlefield Earth* and *Lucky Numbers*); Madonna (*The Next Best Thing*)

For 1999: *Wild Wild West;* Adam Sandler (*Big Daddy*); Heather Donahue (*The Blair Witch Project*)

For 1998: *Burn, Hollywood, Burn!;* Bruce Willis (*Armageddon, Mercury Rising* and *The Siege*); the Spice Girls (*Spiceworld the Movie*)

For 1997: *The Postman;* Kevin Costner (*The Postman*); Demi Moore (*G.I. Jane*)

For 1996: *Striptease;* Tom Arnold (*Big Bully, Carpool* and *The Stupids*); Demi Moore (*The Juror* and *Striptease*)

For 1995: *Showgirls;* Pauly Shore (*Jury Duty*); Elizabeth Berkley (*Showgirls*)

For 1994: *Color of Night;* Kevin Costner (*Wyatt Earp*); Sharon Stone (*Intersection* and *The Specialist*)

For 1993: *Indecent Proposal;* Burt Reynolds (*Cop and a Half*); Madonna (*Body of Evidence*)

For 1992: *Shining Through;* Sylvester Stallone (*Stop! Or My Mom Will Shoot*); Melanie Griffith (*Shining Through* and *A Stranger Among Us*)

For 1991: *Hudson Hawk;* Kevin Costner (*Robin Hood, Prince of Thieves*); Sean Young (*A Kiss Before Dying*)

For 1990: *Adventures of Ford Fairline* tied with *Ghosts Can't Do It;* Andrew Dice Clay (*Adventures of Ford Fairline*); Bo Derek (*Ghosts Can't Do It*)

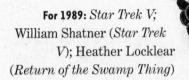

For 1989: *Star Trek V;* William Shatner (*Star Trek V*); Heather Locklear (*Return of the Swamp Thing*)

For 1988: *Cocktail;* Sylvester Stallone (*Rambo III*); Liza Minnelli (*Arthur 2: On the Rocks* and *Rent-A-Cop*)

For 1987: *Leonard: Part 6;* Bill Cosby (*Leonard: Part 6*); Madonna (*Who's That Girl?*)

For 1986: *Howard the Duck* tied with *Under the Cherry Moon;* Prince (*Under the Cherry Moon*); Madonna (*Shanghai Surprise*)

For 1985: *Rambo: First Blood Part II;* Sylvester Stallone (*Rambo: First Blood Part II* and *Rocky IV*); Linda Blair (*Night Patrol, Savage Island* and *Savage Streets*)

For 1984: *Bolero;* Sylvester Stallone (*Rhinestone*); Bo Derek (*Bolero*)

For 1983: *The Lonely Lady;* Christopher Atkins (*A Night in Heaven*); Pia Zadora (*The Lonely Lady*)

For 1982: *Inchon!;* Laurence Olivier (*Inchon!*); Pia Zadora (*Butterfly*)

For 1981: *Mommie Dearest;* Klinton Spillsbury (*Legend of the Lone Ranger*); Bo Derek (*Tarzan, The Ape Man*) tied with Faye Dunaway (*Mommie Dearest*)

For 1980: *Can't Stop the Music;* Neil Diamond (*The Jazz Singer*); Brooke Shields (*The Blue Lagoon*)

Dumb Things People Have Said

"Go back to Liverpool, Mr. Epstein, groups with guitars are out." (Dick Rowe of Decca, rejecting the Beatles)

"Iran is an island of stability in one of the most volatile parts of the world." (President Jimmy Carter, speaking just before the shah was overthrown)

"This picture is going to be one of the biggest white elephants of all time." (Victor Fleming, the director of *Gone With the Wind*, assessing its likely prospects at the box office)

"I'm astounded by people who take eighteen years to write something. That's how long it took that guy to write *Madame Bovary*, and was that ever on the bestseller list?" (Sylvester Stallone)

"Come, come—why, they couldn't hit an elephant at this dist—" (John Sedgwick, American Civil War general, just before he was shot dead)

"**Who could** take that scruffy, arrogant buffoon seriously?" (Eddie Fisher on Richard Burton—just before Burton ran off with Elizabeth Taylor, Fisher's wife)

"**China is** a big country, inhabited by many Chinese." (French president Charles de Gaulle)

"**Smoking kills.** If you're killed, you've lost a very important part of your life." (Brooke Shields)

The Worker's Prayer

"**Grant me** the serenity to accept the things I cannot change, the courage to change the things I cannot accept and the wisdom to hide the bodies of those people I had to kill today because they pissed me off, and also help me to be careful of the toes I step on today, as they may be connected to the butt that I might have to kiss tomorrow."

Friday the 13th

The fear of the number 13—or "triskaidekaphobia" as it's technically known—goes back a long way. According to Scandinavian mythology, there was a banquet in Valhalla into which Loki (the god of strife) intruded—thereby making thirteen guests—and where Balder (the god of light) was murdered. In Christian countries this superstition was confirmed by the Last Supper.

Meanwhile, Friday is considered unlucky because it was the day of the crucifixion and because Adam and Eve ate the forbidden fruit on a Friday and also died on a Friday. Some Buddhists and Brahmins (high-caste Hindus) also consider Friday to be unlucky. In combining superstitions about both Friday and the number thirteen, Friday the 13th is feared as being twice as frightful.

Winston Churchill, the former British prime minister, never traveled on a Friday the 13th unless it was absolutely essential.

Graham Chapman, the late member of the Monty Python team, actually liked Friday the 13ths. Indeed, he arranged to be buried on the thirteenth hour of Friday, October 13, 1989.

Good things that have happened on a Friday the 13th include these: *The Third Man* premiered (January 1950), the Allies recaptured Tobruk (November 1942), and Alfred Dreyfus was restored to the French army and promoted to major (July 1906).

Bad things that have happened on a Friday the 13th include these: a violent earthquake in Turkey killed more than a thousand people (March 1992), a hurricane in Britain left nine people dead (January 1984), and a plane crash left survivors stranded in the Andes without food and compelled them to turn to cannibalism to stay alive (October 1972).

Months that begin on a Sunday will always have a Friday the 13th.

People who were born on a Friday the 13th include Steve Buscemi, Zoe Wanamaker, Howard Keel and Christopher Plummer.

People who have died on a Friday the 13th include Benny Goodman and former U.S. vice president Hubert Humphrey.

Beds and Sleep

We spend something like a third of our lives in bed.

> **Sixty-four percent** of women sleep on the left side of the bed.

An adult sleeping with another adult in a full-size bed—four feet, six inches wide and six feet, two inches long—has less personal space than a baby in a crib.

> **When the Hays Office** censored Hollywood films, there was a series of rules concerning what could and could not be shown on-screen: for example, couples—even married couples—could not be shown in a bed together unless both the man and the woman had at least one foot on the floor.

Hans Christian Andersen, the Danish writer of fairy tales, died falling out of bed (actuarially, the chances of dying by falling out of bed are one in 2 million in a year).

> **In Tallin,** Estonia, couples are not allowed to play chess in bed while making love.

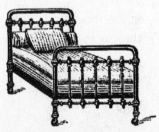

Not only is homosexuality banned in Albania, but two people of the same sex are also banned from sharing a bed—even if they're not homosexual.

The expression "to get out of bed on the wrong side" comes from the nineteenth-century superstition that there was a "right" side (the right) for getting out of bed and a "wrong" side (the left), based, of course, on the traditional fear of anything "left" (*sinister* being the Latin word for left).

King Louis XI of France started the practice of French kings' receiving their courtiers and ministers in bed by introducing *lit de justice* ("bed of justice"), a ceremonial appearance before his parliament of the king lying in bed, with his princes on stools and with great officials standing and lesser ones kneeling.

Mark Twain wrote large parts of *The Adventures of Huckleberry Finn* and *The Adventures of Tom Sawyer* in bed, though he pointed out that working in bed must be very dangerous as so many deaths occur there.

Mae West did all her writing in bed, remarking, "Everybody knows I do my best work in bed."

Robert Louis Stevenson wrote most of *Kidnapped* in bed.

Winston Churchill habitually dictated letters and went through his briefing papers in bed.

Thomas Hobbes, the philosopher, and the writers Edith Wharton, F. Scott Fitzgerald and Marcel Proust all worked in their beds.

When John Denver lost his temper with his then wife, Annie (made famous in "Annie's Song"), he sawed their bed in half.

More than six hundred thousand Americans each year are injured on beds and chairs.

The shortest recorded time taken by one person to make a bed is 28.2 seconds, by Wendy Wall of Sydney, Australia, in 1978; the record time for two people to make a bed is 14 seconds, by Sister Sharon Stringer and Nurse Michelle Benkel at London's Royal Masonic Hospital at the launch of the 1994 edition of *The Guinness Book of Records*.

George Burns once said, "You have to have something to get you out of bed. I can't do anything in bed anyway."

The United States has many sleepy towns: Sleepy Eye (Minnesota), Sleepy Creek (Oregon), Sleeping Beauty Peak (Arizona), Sleepers Bend (California).

According to the philosopher Friedrich Nietzsche, "Sleeping is no mean art. For its sake one must stay awake all day."

Max Kauffmann reckoned that "the amount of sleep required by the average person is about five minutes more," while Fran Lebowitz decided, "Sleep is death without the responsibility."

Insomnia is defined as "a chronic inability to fall asleep or to enjoy uninterrupted sleep," and it affects nearly everyone at some stage. W. C. Fields's cure for insomnia was "Get plenty of sleep."

Famous insomniacs include Elizabeth Taylor, Winona Ryder, Margaret Thatcher, Robbie Williams, Gwyneth Paltrow, Daryl Hannah, Renée Zellweger, Hillary Clinton, Mariah Carey (who claims that she sleeps for just three hours a night), Michelle Pfeiffer (who can't sleep at all some nights), Colin Farrell and Justin Timberlake.

Famous people in history who were insomniacs include Samuel Beckett, Abraham Lincoln, Marilyn Monroe, Spencer Tracy, Vincent van Gogh, Napoleon Bonaparte, Charles Dickens, Cary Grant, Caligula, Marlene Dietrich, W. C. Fields, F. Scott Fitzgerald, Galileo, Hermann Göring and Rudyard Kipling.

Sleepwalking, or somnambulism, is no joke. In 1987 an eleven-year-old American boy, Michael Dixon, was found a hundred miles away from his home after sleepwalking to a freight train and traveling on it from Illinois to Indiana.

Snoring is also no joke—especially for the sleeping partners of sufferers. Great snorers in history have included Beau Brummell, Abraham Lincoln, King George II and Benito Mussolini. "Laugh and the world laughs with you; snore and you sleep alone," declared Anthony Burgess, while Mark Twain wondered why "there ain't no way to find out why a snorer can't hear himself snore."

St. Valentine's Day

St. Valentine was a bishop of Terni who was martyred in Rome in the year 270 but is now omitted from the calendar of saints' days as "probably non-existent."

In 1477 one Margery Brews sent a letter to a man named John Paston addressed "To my right welbelovyd Voluntyne"; this is reckoned to be the oldest known valentine card in existence.

The British send more valentine cards than people in any other country.

People who were born on St. Valentine's Day include Carl Bernstein, Gregory Hines, Meg Tilly and Alan Parker.

People who died on St. Valentine's Day include Captain James Cook, P. G. Wodehouse, John Ehrlichman and the composer of *My Fair Lady*, Frederick Loewe.

Things that have happened on St. Valentine's Day include the opening night of Oscar Wilde's *The Importance of Being Earnest* in 1895 and, of course, the St. Valentine's Day Massacre in 1929.

The Funniest Joke in the World?

In 2002, after much research, British scientists identified what they called the funniest joke in the world. Here it is:

A couple of New Jersey hunters are out in the woods when one of them falls to the ground. He doesn't seem to be breathing; his eyes are rolled back in his head. The other guy whips out his cell phone and calls the emergency services. He gasps to the operator, "My friend is dead! What can I do?" The operator, in a calm, soothing voice, says, "Just take it easy. I can help. First, let's make sure he's dead." There is a silence, and then a shot is heard. The guy's voice comes back on the line. He says, "Okay, now what?"

Star Trek

In all its different incarnations, *Star Trek* has become the most popular form of entertainment of all time. As a result of the different TV series—including *Star Trek: The Next Generation* and a cartoon series—and seven films, *Star Trek* has become a billion-dollar industry, with more merchandise (books, comics, clothes, etc.) sold than any other film or TV series. It is now estimated that an episode of *Star Trek* is transmitted somewhere on earth twenty-four hours a day, 365 days a year.

Given that the original TV series wasn't such a hit—after every season the program's future was in doubt—there weren't many famous guest stars. One exception to this was Joan Collins, who played Edith Keller in the episode "City on the Edge of Forever." This was the one in which Kirk fell in love with a woman (Joan) on earth in the past but was forced to watch her die in a road accident.

"City on the Edge of Forever" and "The Trouble with Tribbles" (the one with all the little furry animals) are acknowledged by most Trekkers to be the best two episodes of *Star Trek*. It is also generally accepted that "Spock's Brain"—in which the great man has his brain stolen—is the stupidest episode.

> **There were** seventy-nine *Star Trek* episodes in its first incarnation. In the pilot, "The Cage," the Captain (Captain Pike) was played by Jeffrey Hunter. When the TV series got the go-ahead, Hunter declined to be in it (rumor has it that his wife advised him against it), and William Shatner was picked instead.

In *Star Trek* the Klingons are the enemy. The Klingons have their own language, and only upper-class Klingons (those serving in the highest levels of the government or the military) speak English. Incredibly, there are now universities where you can study Klingon, and more people in the world speak Klingon than speak the international language Esperanto.

> **Like Leonard Nimoy** (Spock), William Shatner was born in 1931, but his character, Captain Kirk, was born in the year 2233. Even if William Shatner lives to the age of three hundred, he still won't have been "born."

Just as Humphrey Bogart never said, "Play it again, Sam," and James Cagney never said, "You dirty rat," so Captain Kirk never said, "Beam me up, Scottie." He did say, "Beam me up, Mr. Scott" and "Two to beam up, Mr. Scott," but never the most famous (mis)quote from the series.

James Doohan, who played Scottie, was Canadian by birth. The actor was a captain in the Royal Canadian Artillery during World War II, and, along with DeForest Kelley (Dr. McCoy), was the oldest of the *Star Trek* regulars—both having been born in 1920.

Nichelle Nichols, who played Lieutenant Uhura, broke new ground in U.S. television—simply by being a black actress on-screen as an equal with white actors. Nevertheless, she almost quit because her role was limited to a couple of lines per show (e.g., "Getting no reply, Captain," and "Hailing frequencies open, Captain"). She was persuaded to stay by the great civil rights leader Dr. Martin Luther King Jr.

Classic Movies That Didn't Win a Single Oscar Among Them

Bad Day at Black Rock (1955)

The Sixth Sense (1999)

Taxi Driver (1976)

Four Weddings and a Funeral (1994)

Awakenings (1990)

The Elephant Man (1980)

Being John Malkovich (1999)

Brief Encounter (1946)

The Talented Mr. Ripley (1999)

To Be or Not to Be (1942)

Deliverance (1972)

The Magnificent Ambersons (1942)

I Am a Fugitive from a Chain Gang (1932)

The Shawshank Redemption (1994)

Quiz Show (1994)

The Great Escape (1963)

American Graffiti (1973)

A Clockwork Orange (1971)

Top Hat (1935)

Dr. Strangelove, Or: How I Learned to Stop Worrying and Love the Bomb (1964)

Psycho (1960)

It's a Wonderful Life (1946)

12 Angry Men (1957)

The Green Mile (1999)

Vertigo (1958)

Odd Man Out (1947)

Ninotchka (1939)

The Maltese Falcon (1941)

classic movies that didn't win a single oscar among them

Lenny (1974)

Field of Dreams (1989)

The Player (1992)

Rebel Without a Cause (1955)

The Caine Mutiny (1954)

The Great Dictator (1940)

Fatal Attraction (1987)

The China Syndrome (1979)

When Harry Met Sally (1989)

Cat on a Hot Tin Roof (1958)

Rear Window (1954)

Ace in the Hole (1951)

A Star Is Born (1954)

Alfie (1966)

Pretty Woman (1990)

North by Northwest (1959)

Full Metal Jacket (1987)

The Wild Bunch (1969)

A Few Good Men (1992)

Singin' in the Rain (1952)

Amélie (2001)

Serpico (1973)

Classic Movies That Didn't Win a Single Oscar *Nomination* Among Them

The Wild One (1953)

Oliver Twist (1948)

His Girl Friday (1940)

Reservoir Dogs (1992)

The Night of the Hunter (1955)

The Searchers (1956)

Dirty Harry (1971)

The Postman Always Rings Twice (1946)

The 39 Steps (1935)

The Big Sleep (1946)

Sweet Smell of Success (1957)

This Is Spinal Tap (1984)

Kind Hearts and Coronets (1948)

King Kong (1933)

Mean Streets (1973)

A Night at the Opera (1934)

Bringing Up Baby (1938)

Paths of Glory (1957)

Modern Times (1936)

The Lady Vanishes (1939)

Once Upon a Time in America (1984)

All of *Time* Magazine's "Person of the Year" Winners

2005: Bill Gates, Melinda Gates, and Bono

2004: George W. Bush

2003: The American Soldier

2002: The Whistleblowers

2001: Rudolph Giuliani

2000: George W. Bush

1999: Jeff Bezos

1998: Bill Clinton and Kenneth Starr

1997: Andy Grove

1996: Dr. David Ho

1995: Newt Gingrich

1994: Pope John Paul II

1993: The Peacemakers

1992: Bill Clinton

1991: Ted Turner

1990: The Two
George Bushes

1989: Mikhail Gorbachev

1988: Endangered Earth

1987: Mikhail Gorbachev

1986: Corazon Aquino

1985: Deng Xiaoping

1984: Peter Ueberroth

1983: Ronald Reagan and Yuri Andropov

1982: The Computer

1981: Lech Walesa

1980: Ronald Reagan

1979: Ayatollah Khomeini

1978: Teng Hsiao-p'ing

1977: Anwar Sadat

1976: Jimmy Carter

1975: American Women

1974: King Faisal

1973: John Sirica

1972: Richard Nixon and Henry Kissinger

1971: Richard Nixon

1970: Willy Brandt

1969: The Middle Americans

1968: Astronauts Anders, Borman and Lovell

1967: Lyndon Johnson

1966: Twenty-five and Under

1965: General William Westmoreland

1964: Lyndon Johnson

1963: Martin Luther King Jr.

1962: Pope John XXIII

1961: John Kennedy

1960: U.S. Scientists

1959: Dwight Eisenhower

1958: Charles de Gaulle

1957: Nikita Khrushchev

1956: Hungarian Freedom Fighter

1955: Harlow Curtice

1954: John Foster Dulles

1953: Konrad Adenauer

1952: Queen Elizabeth II

1951: Mohammed Mossadegh

1950: American Fighting Man

1949: Winston Churchill

1948: Harry Truman

1947: George Marshall

1946: James Byrnes

1945: Harry Truman

1944: Dwight Eisenhower

1943: George Marshall

1942: Joseph Stalin

1941: Franklin Roosevelt

1940: Winston Churchill

1939: Joseph Stalin

1938: Adolf Hitler

1937: Generalissimo and Madame Chiang Kai-shek

1936: Wallis Simpson

1935: Haile Selassie

1934: Franklin Roosevelt

1933: Hugh Johnson

1932: Franklin Roosevelt

1931: Pierre Laval

1930: Mohandas Gandhi

1929: Owen Young

1928: Walter Chrysler

1927: Charles Lindbergh

Banned Books

The Catcher in the Rye (J. D. Salinger): banned in Boron, California, in 1989 because of the word *goddamn*. This is probably the most famous work of fiction never to have been turned into a feature film.

The Adventures of Tom Sawyer (Mark Twain): banned by several London libraries (in politically correct Labour-controlled boroughs) in the mid-1980s on account of the book's "racism" and "sexism."

Black Beauty (Anna Sewell): banned by the African country Namibia in the 1970s because the government took offense at the "racist" title.

The Scarlet Pimpernel (Baroness Orczy): banned by the Nazis—not because of its language or its theme (though Leslie Howard starred in an anti-Nazi film entitled *Pimpernel Smith*)—but because Baroness Orczy was Jewish. Other authors banned by the Nazis for the same reason included Erich Maria Remarque, Thomas Mann, Sigmund Freud and Marcel Proust. Authors banned by the Nazis because of their political sentiments included Ernest Hemingway, Upton Sinclair and Jack London.

Noddy (Enid Blyton): banned by several British libraries in the 1960s—along with other Enid Blyton books—because they weren't thought to be "good" for children.

The Grapes of Wrath (John Steinbeck): banned from schools in the state of Iowa in 1980 after a parent complained that the classic novel—by the Nobel Prize–winner—was "vulgar and obscene." Steinbeck's other famous novel, *Of Mice and Men*, has also been banned in other U.S. states for similar reasons.

The Joy of Sex (Alex Comfort): banned in Ireland from its publication until 1989 on account of the book's uninhibited approach to sex and relationships. The Irish have done more than their share of banning: All of Steinbeck and Zola's novels were banned in Ireland in 1953 for being "subversive" and/or "immoral." Other books once banned by the Irish include *Brave New World* (Aldous Huxley), *Elmer Gantry* (Sinclair Lewis) and *The Sun Also Rises* (Ernest Hemingway).

On the Origin of Species (Charles Darwin): banned in several U.S. states (especially in the Christian fundamentalist South) through the years—but particularly before World War II—owing to the fact that Darwin didn't accept the Bible's account of Creation. Incredibly, Desmond Morris's *The Naked Ape* has been banned from one or two U.S. libraries on the same basis. Darwin's book was also banned by the USSR because it was "immoral."

My Friend Flicka (Mary O'Hara): banned from schoolchildren's reading lists in Clay County, Florida, in 1990 because the book contains the word *bitch* to describe a female dog.

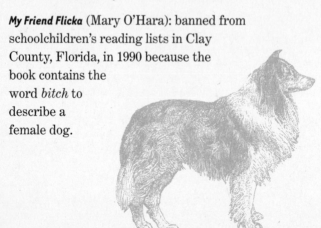

Losing U.S. Presidential and Vice-Presidential Candidates

Year: Presidential Candidate / Vice-Presidential Candidate

2004: John Kerry / John Edwards

2000: Al Gore / Joseph Lieberman

1996: Robert Dole / Jack Kemp

1992: George Bush / Dan Quayle

1988: Michael Dukakis / Lloyd Bentsen

1984: Walter Mondale / Geraldine Ferraro

1980: Jimmy Carter / Walter Mondale

1976: Gerald Ford / Robert Dole

1972: George McGovern / Sargent Shriver

1968: Hubert Humphrey / Edmund Muskie

1964: Barry Goldwater / William Miller

1960: Richard Nixon / Henry Cabot Lodge

1956: Adlai Stevenson / Estes Kefauver

1952: Adlai Stevenson / John Sparkman

1948: Thomas Dewey / Earl Warren

1944: Thomas Dewey / John Bricker

1940: Wendell Wilkie / Charles McNary

1936: Alf Landon / Frank Knox

1932: Herbert Hoover / Charles Curtis

1928: Alfred Smith / Joseph Robinson

1924: John Davis / Charles Bryan

1920: James Cox / Franklin Roosevelt

1916: Charles Hughes / Charles Fairbanks

1912: William Taft / Nicholas Butler

1912: Theodore Roosevelt / Hiram Johnson

1908: William Bryan / John Kern

1904: Alton Parker / Henry Davis

1900: William Bryan / Adlai E. Stevenson

Things from Abroad

Danish pastry, German measles, Brazil nuts, Mexican stand-off, Dutch elm disease, Chinese whispers, Russian roulette, Swiss cheese, Hong Kong flu, Greek urn, Singapore sling, Dutch uncle, Turkish delight, Indian tonic water, French bread, Maltese cross, Italian vermouth, Panama hat, Spanish omelette

Things That Are Brand Names

Jiffy Bag, Plasticine, Hoover, Scotch tape, Jacuzzi, Spam, Formica, Jell-O, Kleenex, Xerox, Baggie

The Last Words of Men About to Be Executed

George Appel (1928) As Appel was being strapped into the electric chair, he said to the witnesses, "Well, folks, you'll soon see a baked Appel."

Thomas Grasso (1995) Before he was given his lethal injection, he complained, "I did not get my SpaghettiOs, I got spaghetti. I want the press to know this."

Sir Walter Raleigh (1618) "So the heart be right, it is no matter which way the head lieth." And then he was beheaded.

James French (1966) On his way to the chair, he said to a newspaper reporter, "I have a terrific headline for you in the morning: 'French Fries.'"

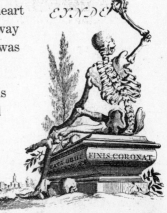

Francis Crowley (1931) "You sons of bitches. Give my love to Mother." Then he was electrocuted.

Neville Heath (1946) Just before being hanged, his last request was for a whiskey. "In the circumstances," he added, "you might make that a double."

Johnny Frank Garrett (1992) Before being lethally injected, he said, "I'd like to thank my family for loving me and taking care of me. And the rest of the world can kiss my ass."

Erskine Childers (1922) He called out to the firing squad, "Take a step forward, lads. It will be easier that way."

Robert Drew (1994) Before being given his lethal injection, he said, "Remember, the death penalty is murder."

Frederick Wood (1963) When Wood was in the electric chair, he said to the assembled company, "Gentlemen, you are about to see the effects of electricity upon wood."

Ned Kelly (1880) The notorious Australian bushwacker's last words as he stood on the scaffold awaiting his hanging were, "Ah well, I suppose it had to come to this. Such is life."

Jimmy Glass (1987) said, "I'd rather be fishing." Then he was electrocuted.

Gerald Chapman (1926) Just before he was hanged, he said, "Death itself isn't dreadful, but hanging seems an awkward way of entering the adventure."

Gary Gilmore (1977) Having campaigned for the right to die, he just said, "Let's do it!"—and the firing squad duly did.

Robert Alton Harris (1992) Before being gassed, he said, "You can be a king or a street sweeper, but everyone dances with the Grim Reaper."

Dr. William Palmer (1856) The British serial killer stood on the gallows and asked the officials, "Are you sure this thing is safe?"

Scrabble

Scrabble was invented in 1931 by Alfred Butts, an unemployed American architect. Butts (who wasn't himself a good Scrabble player and admitted that the game should have had fewer *i*s) originally called the game Lexico. However, both the format and the name were changed many times—later names included Alpha and Criss Cross Words—before the current format was established with the name Scrabble in 1948. The game wasn't commercially successful until 1952, when the chairman of the New York department store Macy's became addicted to it on his vacation. He placed a large order for the game and did a huge promotional campaign. The rest is history.

Scrabble is currently produced in 30 different languages—from Afrikaans to Hebrew, from Japanese and English to Malaysian. In total, more than 100 million games have been sold in 121 countries.

Celebrity Scrabble fans include Brad Pitt, Jennifer Aniston, Will Smith, Robbie Williams, Elizabeth Taylor, Kylie Minogue, Madonna, Sting and Mel Gibson.

The highest number of points that can be achieved on the first turn (when there are no other letters on the board) is 126—using the word *quartzy* or the word *squeezy*. Don't forget that there is a 50-point bonus for using all 7 letters in one go.

The highest score achieved for one word in a competition (i.e., when other people were watching) was 392 for *caziques* down two triple-word scores.

As all good Scrabble players know, there are 109 permissible two-letter words. These include *jo* (a northern sweetheart), *ka* (an attendant spirit), *xi* (a letter in the Greek alphabet) and *qi* (derived from Chinese—means life force).

quartzy

squeezy

The Most Valuable Words You Can Make at Scrabble

Word	Meaning	Score (+ bonus of 50 for using all 7 letters)
QUIZZIFY*	To cause to look odd	31

(N.B. If this were stretched across two triple-word scores, it would total 419 points—including the 50-point bonus and the double-letter bonus for the z)

WHIPJACKA	whining beggar who pretends to be a sailor	29
HIGHJACK	Alternative spelling of hijack	28
JUMBOIZE	To enlarge a ship by adding a prefabricated section	28
BEZIQUES	Plural of card game	28
CAZIQUES	West Indian chiefs	28
QUIZZERY*	Collection of quizzes or information pertaining to quizzes	28
TZADDIQS	In Judaism, leaders or persons of extraordinary piety	28
VIZCACHA	South American burrowing rodent of heavy build	27
ZAMBUCKS	New Zealand or Australian colloquial term for members of St. John's Ambulance Brigade	27

* indicates that the second z is a blank

Characters from Gilbert and Sullivan

Captain Fitzbattleaxe: *Utopia Limited*

Ernest Dummkopf: *The Grand Duke*

Don Alhambra del Bolero: *The Gondoliers*

Sir Marmaduke Pointdextre: *The Sorcerer*

Dick Deadeye: *HMS Pinafore*

Richard Dauntless: *Ruddigore*

Lady Psyche: *Princess Ida*

King Paramount the First: *Utopia Limited*

Sir Despard Murgatroyd: *Ruddigore*

Stupidas: *Thespis*

Beatles Songs and Who or What Inspired Them

"A Hard Day's Night"

Although the title was inspired by a comment from Ringo (as indeed was "Eight Days a Week"), John wrote the song for Julian, his baby son ("But when I get home to you, I find the things that you do, will make me feel all right"). It was for Julian, of course, that Paul wrote "Hey Jude"—to cheer the lad when his parents split.

"Eleanor Rigby"

Paul claimed that he made up the story and the name, but there is a gravestone of a woman named Eleanor Rigby ("Died 10th Oct. 1939 Aged 44 Years. Asleep") in St. Peter's, Woolton—where Paul first met John at a church fair. Could be one of the greatest coincidences of all time.

"Something"

Written by George for his wife, Patti. "Something in the way she moves, attracts me like no other lover." Unfortunately, she had the same effect on Eric Clapton, who wrote "Layla" for her and then married her.

"Lucy in the Sky with Diamonds"

Long after it wouldn't have mattered anyhow, John always insisted that this song had nothing to do with the drug LSD but rather was inspired by a picture painted by a school friend of his son Julian's.

"A Day in the Life"

This song was about lots of things, but the line "He blew his mind out in a car" was inspired by the death in a car of Tara Browne, an Irish heir (he was male, despite the name) who was related to the Guinness family. Browne was friendly with Paul and other members of the rock aristocracy.

"Things We Said Today"

Written by Paul for Jane Asher. "We'll go on and on." Alas not.

"We Can Work It Out"

Once again for Jane Asher. "Try to see it my way," begged Paul, but she wouldn't.

"You've Got to Hide Your Love Away"

Supposedly written by John "for" Brian Epstein. The love that Epstein had to hide was, of course, his homosexuality.

"She's Leaving Home"

Paul read a story in the papers about teenage runaway Melanie Coe. Her father was quoted as saying, "I cannot imagine why she should run away. She has everything here," which has its echo in Paul's line "We gave her everything money could buy." Amazing coincidence: unknown to Paul, he had actually met the young girl when he had presented her with a competition prize on *Ready Steady Go* four years earlier.

"She Said She Said"

Written by John during his acid phase. John got the line "I know what it's like to be dead" when he overheard the actor Peter Fonda talking to George about a near-death childhood experience.

"I Saw Her Standing There"

Like the girl in the song, Iris Caldwell was just seventeen when Paul met her while she was dancing in a nightclub. Iris, whose brother was Liverpool musician Rory Storm, went out with Paul for two years.

"Sexy Sadie"

Famously written by John for the Maharishi Mahesh Yogi, who, John reckons, "made a fool of everyone" by pretending to be pure when really he was a womanizer.

"Dear Prudence"

Written to encourage Prudence Farrow (Mia Farrow's younger sister) to stop meditating so much—"won't you come out to play?"—during the Beatles' time in India.

How the Record for the Mile Has Been Bettered Since Roger Bannister Broke the Four-Minute Barrier

3:59.4 Roger Bannister (Great Britain) Oxford, UK (5/6/54)

3:58.0 John Landy (Australia) Turku, Finland (6/21/54)

3:57.2 Derek Ibbotson (Great Britain) London, UK (7/19/57)

3:54.5 Herb Elliott (Australia) Dublin, Ireland (8/6/58)

3:54.4 Peter Snell (New Zealand) Wanganui, New Zealand (1/27/62)

3:54.1 Peter Snell Auckland, New Zealand (11/17/64)

3:53.6 Michel Jazy (France) Rennes, France (6/9/65)

3:51.3 Jim Ryun (U.S.A.) Berkeley, U.S.A. (7/17/66)

3:51.1 Jim Ryun Bakersfield, U.S.A. (7/23/67)

3:51.0 Filbert Bayi (Tanzania) Kingston, Jamaica (5/17/75)

3:49.4 John Walker (New Zealand) Gothenburg, Sweden (8/12/75)

3:49.0 Sebastian Coe (Great Britain) Oslo, Norway (7/17/79)

3:48.8 Steve Ovett (Great Britain) Oslo, Norway (7/1/80)

3:48.53 Sebastian Coe Zurich, Switzerland (8/19/81)

3:48.40 Steve Ovett Koblenz, Germany (8/25/81)

3:47.33 Sebastian Coe Brussels, Belgium (8/28/81)

3:46.32 Steve Cram (Great Britain) Oslo, Norway (7/27/85)

3:44.39 Noureddine Morceli (Algeria) Rieti, Italy (9/5/93)

3:43.13 Hicham El Guerrouj (Morocco) Rome, Italy (7/7/99)

The Titles of All *Monty Python's Flying Circus* TV Programs

SEASON 1
(first aired between October 5, 1969, and January 11, 1970)

1. "Whither Canada?"

2. "Sex and Violence"

3. "How to Recognize Different Types of Tree from Quite a Long Way Away"

4. "Owl-Stretching Time"

5. "Man's Crisis of Identity in the Latter Half of the Twentieth Century"

6. "The BBC Entry to the Zinc Stoat of Budapest"

7. "You're No Fun Any More"

8. "Full Frontal Nudity"

9. "The Ant, an Introduction"

10. "Untitled"

11. "The Royal Philharmonic Orchestra Goes to the Bathroom"

12. "The Naked Ant"

13. "Intermission"

SEASON 2
(first aired between September 15, 1970, and December 22, 1970)

1. "Dinsdale"

2. "The Spanish Inquisition"

3. "Show 5"

4. "The Buzz Aldrin Show"

5. "Live from the Grill-o-Mat Snack Bar"

6. "School Prizes"

7. "The Attila the Hun Show"

8. "Archaeology Today"

9. "How to Recognize Different Parts of the Body"

10. "Scott of the Antarctic"

11. "How Not to Be Seen"

12. "Spam"

13. "Royal Episode 13"

SEASON 3
(first aired between October 19, 1972, and January 18, 1973)

1. "Whicker's World"

2. "Mr. & Mrs. Brian Norris's Ford Popular"

3. "The Money Programme"

4. "Blood, Devastation, Death, War and Horror"

5. "The All-England Summarize Proust Competition"

6. "The War Against Pornography"

7. "Salad Days"

8. "The Cycling Tour"

9. "The Nude Man"

10. "E. Henry Tripshaw's Disease"

11. "Dennis Moore"

12. "A Book at Bedtime"

13. "Grandstand"

SEASON 4
(first aired between October 31, 1974, and December 5, 1974)

1. "The Golden Age of Ballooning"

2. "Michael Ellis"

3. "Light Entertainment War"

4. "Hamlet"

5. "Mr. Neutron"

6. "Party Political Broadcast"

Titles Considered Instead of *Monty Python's Flying Circus* for *Monty Python's Flying Circus*

It's . . .

A Horse, a Bucket and a Spoon

A Toad-Elevating Moment

Bun, Whackett, Buzzard, Stubble and Boot

Sex and Violence

Owl-Stretching Time

1 2 3

Vaseline Parade

The Horrible Earnest Megapode

The Plastic Mac Show

The Venus de Milo Panic Show

The Year of the Stoat

The Nose Show

Names Walt Disney Allegedly Considered and Rejected for Snow White's Dwarfs

Gloomy, Wheezy, Shirty, Sniffy, Woeful, Weepy, Lazy, Snoopy, Puffy, Shorty, Baldy, Biggo-Ego, Burpy, Gabby, Jumpy, Nifty, Stubby, Stuffy

Souvenirs from the James Bond Films

James Bond Children's Pink Slippers (1979), James Bond Underpants (1983), James Bond Thermos Flask (1965), James Bond Moon Boots (1981), James Bond Soap (1985), James Bond Moon Buggy (1971), James Bond Lunch Box (1965), James Bond Socks (1988), James Bond Pencil Box (1985), James Bond Spear Gun (1965)

The First European Countries to Have McDonald's

Germany (Munich, 1971)

Holland (Voorburg, 1972)

Sweden (Stockholm, 1973)

UK (Woolwich, London, 1974)

Switzerland (Geneva, 1975)

Ireland (Dublin, 1977)

Austria (Vienna, 1977)

Belgium (Brussels, 1978)

France (Strasbourg, 1979)

Spain (Madrid, 1981)

Couples Who Divorced and Then Remarried

Elizabeth Taylor and Richard Burton

Melanie Griffith and Don Johnson

Elliott Gould and Jenny Bogart

Sarah Miles and Robert Bolt

Robert Wagner and Natalie Wood

Dorothy Parker and Alan Campbell

George Peppard and Elizabeth Ashley

Jane Wyman and Fred Karger

Dionne Warwick and Bill Elliott

Paul Hogan and Noelene Edwards

Kurt Weill and Lotte Lenya

José Ferrer and Rosemary Clooney

George C. Scott and Colleen Dewhurst

Dennis Wilson and Karen Lamm

Milton Berle and Joyce Matthews

Billy Rose and Joyce Matthews

Neil and Diane Simon

Andy and Kate Summers

Alexander Solzhenitsyn and Natalya Reshtovskaya

Art and Jean Carney

Note also: Cher's parents married and divorced each other three times

Men Who Fell in Love with Their Wife's Sister

Charles Dickens, George Sanders (after divorcing Zsa Zsa Gabor, he married her sister Magda), Peter Paul Rubens (did it the other way around—marrying the sister, Helena, of Suzanne, his former mistress), Peter Bogdanovich (also did it the other way around—marrying the sister, Louise, of his murdered lover, Dorothy Stratton), King Henry VIII (also did it the other way around—marrying the sister, Anne Boleyn, of his erstwhile lover, Mary), Wolfgang Mozart, Stavros Niarchos, Sigmund Freud

People Who Married Their Cousin

Franklin D. Roosevelt; Albert Einstein; Lewis Carroll; Mary, Queen of Scots; Queen Victoria; Satyajit Ray; Charles Darwin; Saddam Hussein; King Olav V of Norway; Karen Blixen; Catherine the Great; André Gide; H. G. Wells; Edgar Allan Poe (whose bride was just thirteen); Jerry Lee Lewis (whose bride was also just thirteen)

People Who Were Betrothed Very Quickly

Muhammad Ali—in 1964 he met Sonji Roi and proposed to her on the same day; they married forty-two days later.

Michael Douglas—in 1977 he met Diandra Luker at Jimmy Carter's presidential inauguration. They spent two days in his Washington hotel room, he proposed after nine days, and they married six weeks later.

Pamela Anderson—in 1995 she and Tommy Lee decided to marry after a five-day courtship.

Charlie Sheen—in 1995 he married Donna Peele after a six-week courtship.

Julia Roberts—in 1993 she married Lyle Lovett after a three-week romance.

Kate Jackson—in 1978 she married Andrew Stevens after a six-week courtship.

Drew Barrymore—in 1994 she married Jeremy Thomas after a six-week courtship.

Shannen Doherty—in 1993 she married Ashley Hamilton after a two-week romance.

John Major—in 1970 he and Norma Wagstaff decided to marry after just three weeks.

Couples Who Had Open Marriages

Harold and Grace Robbins

Bertrand Russell and Dora Black

Carl and Emma Jung

John F. and Jacqueline Kennedy

Leonard and Virginia Woolf

Salvador and Gala Dalí

Lord Louis and Lady Edwina Mountbatten

Dmitri and Nina Shostakovich

Gary and Veronica (Rocky) Cooper

Horatio and Fanny Nelson

Marlene Dietrich and Rudolf Sieber

Lyndon and Lady Bird Johnson

People Who Committed Bigamy

Rudolph Valentino, King George III, Anaïs Nin, Judy Garland (unwittingly married Mark Herron in 1964 when she was still married to Sid Luft).

It is also claimed that John F. Kennedy married a Palm Beach socialite in 1947 and was still married to her in 1953 when he married Jacqueline Bouvier.

Men Who Married Their Secretary

T. S. Eliot, Burt Lancaster, Fyodor Dostoyevsky, Thomas Hardy

People Who Never Married

Greta Garbo, Isaac Newton, Florence Nightingale, Ludwig van Beethoven, Cecil Rhodes, Frederic Chopin, Queen Elizabeth I, Henri de Toulouse-Lautrec, Jane Austen, Louisa May Alcott, Giacomo Casanova, Lillian Gish, P. L. Travers, George Gershwin, David Hume, John Locke, Jean-Paul Sartre, René Descartes, Immanuel Kant, Friedrich Nietzsche, Philip Larkin, Patricia Highsmith, Adam Smith, Edgar Degas, Maria Montessori, Edward Lear, Benny Hill, Stendhal, Johannes Brahms, Voltaire, Coco Chanel, Vitas Gerulaitis

People Who Married 9 Times

Mike Love, Pancho Villa, Zsa Zsa Gabor

People Who Married 8 Times

Elizabeth Taylor (twice to the same man), Mickey Rooney, Alan Jay Lerner, Artie Shaw

People Who Married 7 Times

Lana Turner, Richard Pryor, Barbara Hutton, Claude Rains, Stan Laurel (three times to the same woman), Jennifer O'Neill, Larry King

People Who Married 6 Times

Rex Harrison, Johnny Weissmuller, Gloria Swanson, Hedy Lamarr, Norman Mailer, King Henry VIII, Harold Robbins, Steve Earle, Jerry Lee Lewis, David Merrick (twice to the same woman)

People Who Married 5 Times

Tony Curtis, Danielle Steel, James Cameron, Billy Bob Thornton, Martin Scorsese, Joan Collins, Stavros Niarchos, David Lean, Ernest Borgnine, George C. Scott (twice to the same woman), George Peppard (twice to the same woman), John Huston, J. Paul Getty, Ginger Rogers, Rue McClanahan, Victor Mature, Eva Gabor, Judy Garland, Henry Fonda, Jane Wyman (twice to the same man), George Foreman, Rita Hayworth, Ingmar Bergman, Tammy Wynette, Clark Gable, Veronica Lake, Richard Burton (twice to the same woman)

People Who Married 4 Times

Frank Sinatra, Stockard Channing, Jason Robards, Ethel Merman, Doris Day, André Previn, Merle Oberon, Dennis Hopper, Janet Leigh, Ernest Hemingway, Barry Humphries, John Derek, David Soul, Donald Pleasence, Liza Minnelli, Charlie Chaplin, George Sanders, Paulette Goddard, Peggy Lee, Bette Davis, Al Jolson, Jane Seymour, Michael Crichton, Peter Sellers, Christina Onassis, Lawrence Durrell, Yul Brynner, Leslie Charteris, Bertolt Brecht, Lionel Barrymore, Melanie Griffith (twice to the same man), Joan Fontaine, Erica Jong, Humphrey Bogart, Cary Grant, Christie Brinkley,

Madeleine Carroll, William Shatner, Joan Crawford, Connie Francis, Mao Tse-tung, Lindsay Wagner, Dinah Sheridan, Brigitte Bardot, Dudley Moore, Eddie Fisher, Burgess Meredith

Men Who Married Older Women

Raymond Chandler (his wife, Pearl Bowen, was 17 years older)

Clark Gable (both of his first wives were considerably older—first wife, Josephine Dillon, was 17 years older)

Benjamin Disraeli (his wife, Mary Wyndham Lewis, was 12 years older)

William Shakespeare (his wife, Anne Hathaway, was 7 years older)

Roger Moore (his second wife, Dorothy Squires, was 12 years older)

Women Who Married Younger Men

Sarah Bernhardt (her only husband was 11 years younger)

Martha Raye (married a man, Mark Harris, 23 years younger)

Colette (her third husband was 17 years younger)

Elizabeth Taylor (married a man, Larry Fortensky, 20 years younger)

Edith Piaf (married a man, Theo Sarapo, 20 years younger)

Merle Oberon (married a man, Robert Wolders, 25 years younger)

Jennie Churchill (married George Cornwallis-West, who was 20 years younger, and Montagu Porch, who was 23 years younger)

Sian Phillips (married Robin Sachs, who is 17 years younger)

Kate Jackson (she twice married men who were 6 years younger)

Joanna Lumley (her husband, Stephen Barlow, is 8 years younger)

Ruth Gordon (her husband, Garson Kanin, was 16 years younger)

Isadora Duncan (her husband, Sergei Esenin, was 17 years younger)

Helena Rubenstein (her husband, Prince Artchil Gourielli-Tchkonia, was 20 years younger)

Joan Collins (her husband, Percy Gibson, is 32 years younger)

People Who Married at the Age of 13

Josephine Baker, Loretta Lynn, Mohandas Gandhi, June Havoc

People Who Married at the Age of 14

Marie Antoinette, Jerry Lee Lewis, Janet Leigh (eloped—the marriage was later annulled)

People Who Married at the Age of 15

Mary, Queen of Scots; Eva Bartok; Annie Oakley; Fanny Brice

People Who Married at the Age of 16

Dolores del Rio, Plácido Domingo, Marilyn Monroe, Catherine the Great, Joan Bennett, Sandra Dee, Tom Jones, Doris Day, Linda Thorson

Couples Who Married in Las Vegas

Ursula Andress and John Derek

John and Bo Derek

Melanie Griffith and Don Johnson (the first time)

Sheena Easton and Tim Delarm

George Clooney and Talia Balsam (by an Elvis impersonator)

Paul Newman and Joanne Woodward

Clint Eastwood and Dina Ruiz

Frank Sinatra and Mia Farrow

Natasha Henstridge and Damian Chapa

Michael Caine and Shakira Baksh

Nicolas Cage and Patricia Arquette

Joan Collins and Peter Holm

Richard Gere and Cindy Crawford

Demi Moore and Bruce Willis

Gabriel Byrne and Ellen Barkin

Sylvia Kristel and Alan Turner

Dudley Moore and Brogan Lane

Elvis Presley and Priscilla Beaulieu (but not by an Elvis impersonator)

Richard and Sally Burton

Brigitte Bardot and Gunther Sachs

Jane Russell and Robert Waterfield

Milla Jovovich and Luc Besson

Bette Midler and Martin von Haselberg (by an Elvis impersonator)

Angelina Jolie and Billy Bob Thornton

Engagements That Didn't Lead to Marriage

Brad Pitt and Gwyneth Paltrow

Audrey Hepburn and James Hanson

Jimmy Connors and Chris Evert

Lauren Bacall and Frank Sinatra

Julia Roberts and Kiefer Sutherland

David Frost and Diahann Carroll

Lucille Ball and Broderick Crawford

The Honorable Julia Stonor and
King George V (when he
was Duke of York)
(because she was a
Catholic)

Naomi Campbell and Adam
Clayton

Greta Garbo and John Gilbert (the engagement ended
on the wedding day—she stood him up at the altar)

Paul McCartney and Jane Asher

Claudia Schiffer and David Copperfield

Johnny Depp and Winona Ryder

Liza Minnelli and Desi Arnaz Jr.

Roger Vadim and Catherine Deneuve

Bryan Ferry and Jerry Hall

Scott Baio and Pamela Anderson

Ben Stiller and Jeanne Tripplehorn

Alyssa Milano and Scott Wolf

Cameron Diaz and Jared Leto

Demi Moore and Emilio Estevez

Sean Penn and Elizabeth McGovern

Sela Ward and Peter Weller

Laura Dern and Jeff Goldblum

Minnie Driver and Josh Brolin

Dan Aykroyd and Carrie Fisher

Marriage Proposals That Were Turned Down

Ernest Hemingway's proposal to Gertrude Stein

The Duke of Westminster's proposal to Coco Chanel

Howard Hughes's proposal to Susan Hayward

James Stewart's proposal to Olivia de Havilland

Marriages That Lasted Less Than 6 Months

Eva Bartok and William Wordsworth (less than 1 day—after the wedding ceremony)

Giuseppe Garibaldi and Giuseppina Raimondi (less than 1 day)

Jean Arthur and Julian Anker (1 day)

Katherine Mansfield and George Mansfield (1 day)

Rudolph Valentino and Jean Acker (1 day)

Adolf Hitler and Eva Braun (1 day)

Robin Givens and Svetozar Marinkovic (1 day)

Fanny Brice and Frank White (3 days)

John Heard and Margot Kidder (6 days)

Dennis Hopper and Michelle Phillips (1 week)

Cher and Gregg Allman (9 days)

Catherine Oxenberg and Robert Evans (12 days)

Patty Duke and Michael Tell (2 weeks)

Carole Landis and Irving Wheeler (3 weeks)

Germaine Greer and Paul du Feu (3 weeks)

Katharine Hepburn and Ludlow Ogden Smith (3 weeks)

Shannen Doherty and Ashley Hamilton (3 weeks)

Gloria Swanson and Wallace Beery (3 weeks)

John Milton and Mary Powell (1 month)

Mike Oldfield and Diana Fuller (1 month)

Jane Wyman and Eugene Wyman (1 month)

Greer Garson and Edward Snelson (5 weeks)

George Brent and Constance Worth (5 weeks)

Jean Peters and Stuart Cramer (5 weeks)

Drew Barrymore and Jeremy Thomas (6 weeks)

Nicolas Cage and Lisa Marie Presley (3 months)

P. J. O'Rourke and Amy Lumet (3 months)

Frank Lloyd Wright and Miriam Noel (3 months)

Joanna Lumley and Jeremy Lloyd (4 months)

Colin Farrell and Amelia Warner (4 months)

Charlie Sheen and Donna Peele (5 months)

Carole Landis and Willie Hunts Jr. (5 months)

Sylvia Kristel and Alan Turner (5 months)

People Who Married Their Ex-Spouse's Relative

Cleopatra married Ptolemy XIII and then, when he died, his brother Ptolemy XIV.

George Sanders married the Gabor sisters, Zsa Zsa and Magda.

Barbara Cartland married the McCorquodale cousins.

Gloria Grahame's second husband was the film director Nicholas Ray; her fourth husband was his son, Tony.

Men Who Were Virgins on Their Wedding Day

Victor Hugo (did it nine times on his wedding night), Tiny Tim, Laurence Olivier, Alfred Hitchcock, George S. Kaufman, Dr. Benjamin Spock, Ronan Keating

The Three German Reichs

The First Reich was the Holy Roman Empire (962–1806)

The Second Reich was the German Empire
(1871–1918)

The Third Reich was the Nazi Empire (1933–45)

Things Invented or Discovered by Americans

Lightning rod (1752)

Bifocals (1760)

Cotton gin (1793)

Revolver (1835)

Telegraph (1837)

Vulcanization of rubber (1839)

Fiberglass (1839)

Ether as a human anesthetic (1842)

Sewing machine (1846)

Safety pin (1849)

Bessemer converter (1851)

Cylinder lock (1851)

Elevator (1852)

Condensed milk (1853)

Oil well (1859)

Machine gun (1862)

Aluminum manufacture (1866)

Typewriter (1867)

Air brake (1868)

Vacuum cleaner (manual) (1869)

Barbed wire (1873)

Earmuffs (1873)

Denim jeans (1874)

Carpet sweeper (1876)

Telephone (1876)

Phonograph (1877)

Mechanical cash register (1879)

Saccharin (1879)

Lightbulb (1880)

Electric fan (1882)

Fountain pen (1884)

Electric transformer (1885)

Coca-Cola (1886)

Handheld camera (1888)

Automatic telephone exchange (1889)

Jukebox (1889)

Zipper (1891)

AC electric generator (1892)

AC electric motor (1892)

Paper matchbook (1892)

Motion pictures (1893)

Escalator (1894)

Electric stove (1896)

Pepsi-Cola (1898)

Tractor (1900)

Safety razor (1901)

Gyrocompass (1905)

Electric washing machine (1906)

Vacuum cleaner (upright) (1907)

Electric toaster (1908)

Bakelite (1910)

Air-conditioning (1911)

Aircraft autopilot (1912)

Moving assembly line (1913)

False eyelashes (1916)

Automatic rifle (1918)

Bulldozer (1923)

Hand-held movie camera (1923)

Frozen food (1924)

Liquid-fueled rocket (1926)

Electric induction (1928)

Electric razor (1928)

Car radio (1929)

Scotch tape (1929)

Cyclotron (1931)

Defibrillator (1932)

FM radio (1933)

Nylon (1935)

Richter scale (1935)

Xerography (1938)

Single-rotor helicopter (1939)

Teflon (1943)

Electronic computer (1946)

Microwave oven (1947)

Radiocarbon dating (1947)

Transistor (1947)

Polaroid camera (1948)

Oral contraceptive (1951)

Polio vaccine (1952)

Video recorder (1952)

Measles vaccine (1953)

Nuclear submarine (1955)

Internal heart pacemaker (1957)

Superconductivity (1957)

Laser (1960)

Industrial robot (1962)

Pull-tab opener (1963)

Quasars (1963)

Electronic musical synthesizer (1965)

Quarks (1967)

Bar codes for retail use (1970)

CD (1972)

Electronic mail (1972)

Personal computer (1976)

Implantable defibrillator (1980)

Permanent artificial heart implant (1982)

Things That Britain Gave to the World

Mariner's compass (1187)

Slide rule (1621)

Pressure cooker (1679)

Match (1680)

Kitchen range (seventeenth century)

Vasectomy (seventeenth century)

Machine gun (1718)

Chronometer (1735)

Sandwich (1760)

Modern flush toilet (1775)

Power loom (1785)

Gas lighting (1792)

Piggy bank (eighteenth century)

Clothes washer and dryer (1800s)

Locomotive (1804)

Photographic lens (1812)

Electromagnet (1824)

Modern rainwear (1830)

Lawn mower (1830)

Computer (1835)

Photography (on paper) (1838)

Postage stamp (1840)

Bicycle (1840)

Travel agency (1841)

Ship's metal hull and propeller (1844)

Pneumatic tire (for buses) (1845)

Glider (1853)

Steel (production) (1854)

Refrigerator (1855)

Linoleum (1860)

Color photography (1861)

Telegraph (transatlantic cable) (1866)

Stapler (1868)

Vending machine (1883)

Pneumatic tire (for bicycles) (1888)

Thermos (1892)

Loudspeaker (1900)

Car disc brakes (1902)

Telephone booth (1903)

Geiger counter (1908)

Stainless steel (1913)

Tank (1916)

Turbojet (1928)

Decompression chamber (1929)

Food processor (1947)

Integrated circuit (1952)

Hovercraft (1955)

Acrylic paint (1964)

CAT scanner (1972)

Test-tube babies (1978)

Genetic fingerprinting (1987)

Note also: soccer, the railway, tennis, sell-by dates on food, the disposable diaper, airline meals, the underground, the custom of embracing under the mistletoe, package tours, garden cities, the hearse, Christmas cards, the miniskirt, punk rock, cricket

Things Invented by the French

The suit (eighteenth century), the tie (seventeenth century), aluminum ware (early nineteenth century), aspirin (1853), the coffeepot (1800), the handkerchief (fifteenth century), the Christmas cracker (nineteenth century), the sewing machine (1830), Teflon utensils (1954), wallpaper (fifteenth century)

Actual Products

Sor Bits (Danish mints), **Krapp** (Scandinavian toilet paper), **Grand Dick** (French red wine), **Nora Knackers** (Norwegian biscuits), **Moron** (Italian wine), **Mukki** (Italian yogurt), **Cock** (French deodorant), **Plopp** (Swedish toffee bar), **Bum** (Turkish biscuits), **Donkee Basterd Suker** (Dutch sugar), **Zit** (Greek soft drink), **Bimbo Bread** (South America), **Craps Chocolate** (France), **Darkie Toothpaste** (Taiwan), **Pschitt** (French soft drink), **Homo-Milk** (Canada)

Unintentionally Funny (Actual) Newspaper Headlines

CAUSE OF AIDS FOUND—SCIENTISTS

LAWYERS GIVE POOR FREE LEGAL ADVICE

MAN FOUND BEATEN, ROBBED BY POLICE

JUVENILE COURT TO TRY SHOOTING DEFENDANT

TRAFFIC DEAD RISE SLOWLY

SHOT OFF WOMAN'S LEG HELPS NICKLAUS TO 66

SQUAD HELPS DOG BITE VICTIM

DRUNK GETS
NINE MONTHS
IN VIOLIN
CASE

DOCTOR TESTIFIES
IN HORSE SUIT

THUGS EAT, THEN ROB
PROPRIETOR

CITY MAY IMPOSE MANDATORY
TIME FOR PROSTITUTION

ENRAGED COW INJURES
FARMER WITH AXE

GRANDMOTHER OF EIGHT MAKES HOLE IN ONE

FARMER BILL DIES IN HOUSE

DEFENDANT'S SPEECH ENDS IN LONG SENTENCE

WHY YOU WANT SEX CHANGES WITH AGE

AMERICAN SHIPS HEAD TO LIBYA

NEW VACCINE MAY CONTAIN RABIES

BLIND WOMAN GETS NEW KIDNEY FROM DAD SHE HASN'T
SEEN IN YEARS

HOSPITALS SUED BY SEVEN FOOT DOCTORS

KICKING BABY CONSIDERED TO BE HEALTHY

DEADLINE PASSES FOR STRIKING POLICE

BOYS CAUSE AS MANY PREGNANCIES AS GIRLS

SUDDEN RUSH TO HELP PEOPLE OUT OF WORK

SAFETY EXPERTS SAY SCHOOL BUS PASSENGERS SHOULD BE
BELTED

CEMETERY ALLOWS PEOPLE TO BE BURIED BY THEIR
PETS

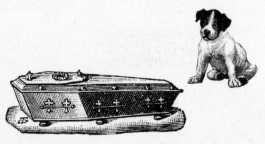

ANTIQUE STRIPPER TO DEMONSTRATE WARES AT STORE

ALEXANDER HOPING PAST IS BEHIND HIM

FLAMING TOILET SEAT CAUSES EVACUATION AT HIGH SCHOOL

MINERS REFUSE TO WORK AFTER DEATH

LUNG CANCER IN WOMEN MUSHROOMS

GENETIC ENGINEERING SPLITS SCIENTISTS

HALF OF ALL CHILDREN TESTED SCORED BELOW AVERAGE

LIVING TOGETHER LINKED TO DIVORCE

STOLEN PAINTING FOUND BY TREE

MAN HELD OVER GIANT L.A. BRUSH FIRE

KIDS MAKE NUTRITIOUS SNACKS

DENTIST RECEIVES PLAQUE

MAN ROBS, THEN KILLS HIMSELF

PROSTITUTES APPEAL TO POPE

POLICE SEARCH FOR WITNESSES TO ASSAULT

Firsts

The world's first traffic island was installed—at his own expense—by Colonel Pierrepoint outside his London club; he was killed crossing over to it.

The first ready-to-eat breakfast cereal was Shredded Wheat in 1893 (it beat Kellogg's Corn Flakes by just five years).

The first scientifically planned slimming diet was devised in 1862 by Dr. Harvey, an ear specialist, for an overweight undertaker (incidentally, dieting was initially something that only men tended to do—women didn't start to do it until they stopped wearing figure-altering corsets).

The first dry cleaning was done in 1849 by a Monsieur Jolly-Bellin of France, who discovered the process by mistake when he upset a lamp over a newly laundered tablecloth and found that the part that was covered with alcohol from the lamp was cleaner than the rest.

The first ice pop dates back to 1923, when lemonade salesman Frank Epperson left a glass of lemonade with a spoon in it on a windowsill one very cold night: the next morning the ice pop was born.

Steven Seagal was the first non-Asian to successfully open a martial-arts academy in Japan.

Groucho Marx ate his first bagel at the age of 81.

Steven Spielberg directed the very first episode of *Columbo*.

Courteney Cox was the first person on U.S. TV ever to use the word *period*—in an ad for Tampax.

Harry Houdini was the first man to fly a plane in Australia—in 1910.

Jimmy Carter was the first president to have been born in a hospital.

The first man to fly over the North Pole—and indeed the South Pole—was called Dickie Byrd.

Gustav Mahler composed his first piece of music at the age of four, Sergei Prokofiev composed his first piece of music aged five, and Wolfgang Mozart was just eight when he composed his first symphony.

The first song Bruce Springsteen ever learned to play on the guitar was The Rolling Stones' "It's All Over Now."

Barbra Streisand's first performance was as a chocolate chip cookie.

Peter Sellers was the first male to be featured on the cover of *Playboy*.

The first duplicating machine was invented by James Watt, the inventor of the steam engine, in 1778 (patented in 1780), to help him with all the copying he had to do for his steam-engine business.

The first member of the British royal family ever to leave home for a haircut was Queen Elizabeth II. It was in Malta back in the days when she was a princess, and she is said to have enjoyed the experience.

Cuba Gooding Jr.'s first job was as a dancer for Lionel Richie at the 1984 Los Angeles Olympics.

Harrison Ford's first film role was as a bellboy in the 1966 film *Dead Heat on a Merry-Go-Round*, and he had to say, "Paging Mr. Ellis" (Ellis being James Coburn).

Proverbs That Are Clearly Not True

An apple a day keeps the doctor away.

You can't judge a book by its cover.

You can't have your cake and eat it, too.

The best things in life are free.

Every cloud has a silver lining.

Ask no questions and you will be told no lies.

Barking dogs seldom bite.

There's no accounting for taste.

The race is not to the swift.

It never rains but it pours.

People Who Were Born on Significant Days in History

Cuba Gooding Jr.—the day that Christiaan Barnard performed his second heart transplant

Michael Crawford—the day that Burma was invaded by the Japanese

Stefan Edberg—the day that Indira Gandhi became Indian prime minister

Emma Bunton (Baby Spice)—the day that Concorde made its first commercial flight (to Bahrain)

Jean Simmons—the day that Leon Trotsky was expelled from the USSR

Terry Jones—the day that Vidkun Quisling became prime minister of Norway

Alice Cooper—the day that Ceylon gained its independence

Robbie Williams—the day that Alexander Solzhenitsyn was expelled from the USSR

John McEnroe—the day that Fidel Castro became prime minister of Cuba

Alan Rickman—the day that the Indian navy mutinied

115

Lee Evans—the day that Muhammad Ali first became world heavyweight champion

Mickey Spillane—the day that Moscow became the capital of Russia

Gary Oldman—the day that the London Planetarium opened

Ayrton Senna—the day that the Sharpeville massacre took place in South Africa

David Frost—the day that Italy invaded Albania

Bianca Jagger—the day that the Germans surrendered in World War II

Lance Bass—the day that Margaret Thatcher became British prime minister

Bob Dylan—the day that the *Bismarck* sank the *Hood*

Stevie Nicks—the day that apartheid began in South Africa

Helena Bonham Carter—the day that Guyana became independent

Craig Stadler—the day that Queen Elizabeth II was crowned

Ice Cube—the day that Georges Pompidou was elected French president

Mike Tyson—the day that U.S. bombs hit Hanoi for the first time

Olivia de Havilland—the day that the first Battle of the Somme began

Tom Cruise—the day that French rule in Algeria ended

O. J. Simpson—the day that Princess Elizabeth's engagement to Prince Philip was announced

Nelson Mandela—the day that the second Battle of the Marne was fought

Raymond Chandler—the day that John Dunlop applied to patent a pneumatic tire

Salvador Allende—the day that the FBI was created

Geri Halliwell—the day that Idi Amin ordered the expulsion of 50,000 Asians from Uganda

Steve Martin—the day that Japan surrendered (VJ Day)

Lily Tomlin—the day that Germany invaded Poland

Keith Duffy—the day that the Watergate trial started

Kate Winslet—the day that Niki Lauda became world racing champion

Joan Plowright—the day of the Wall Street crash

Stubby Kaye—the day that World War I ended

Frank Sinatra—the day that the Germans built the first all-metal airplane

The Only Countries to Have Won the Wimbledon Men's Singles Title

UK—35 wins (the most recent: Fred Perry in 1936)

U.S.A.—33 wins (the most recent: Pete Sampras in 2000)

Australia—21 wins (the most recent: Lleyton Hewitt in 2002)

France—7 wins (the most recent: Yvon Petra in 1946)

Sweden—7 wins (the most recent: Stefan Edberg in 1990)

New Zealand—4 wins (the most recent: Tony Wilding in 1913)

Germany—4 wins (the most recent: Michael Stich in 1991)

Spain—1 win (Manuel Santana in 1966)

Czechoslovakia—1 win (Jan Kodes in 1973)

Holland—1 win (Richard Krajicek in 1996)

Croatia—1 win (Goran Ivanisevic in 2001)

Switzerland—2 wins (Roger Federer in 2003 and 2004)

Note: Jaroslav Drobny won the men's title in 1954 representing Egypt. He was in fact Czech, and later became British.

Wonderfully Named Charles Dickens Characters

Doctor Neeshawts (*The Mudfog Papers*), Oswald Pardiggle (*Bleak House*), Paul Sweedlepipe (*Martin Chuzzlewit*), Doctor Soemup (*The Mudfog Papers*), Mortimer Knag (*Nicholas Nickleby*), Augustus Moddle (*Martin Chuzzlewit*), Quebec Bagnet (*Bleak House*), Simon Tappertit (*Barnaby Rudge*), Mercy Pecksniff (*Martin Chuzzlewit*), Morleena Kenwigs (*Nicholas Nickleby*), Chevy Slyme (*Martin Chuzzlewit*), Dick Swiveller (*The Old Curiosity Shop*), Conkey Chickweed (*Oliver Twist*), Sophy Wackles (*The Old Curiosity Shop*), Minnie Meagles (*Little Dorrit*), Canon Crisparkle (*The Mystery of Edwin Drood*), Peepy Jellyby (*Bleak House*), Nicodemus Boffin (*Our Mutual Friend*), Count Smorltork (*The Pickwick Papers*)

People Who Had Bad Adolescent Acne

Dustin Hoffman, Victoria Beckham, Jennifer Capriati, Jim Henson, Jack Nicholson, Janis Joplin, Mike Myers, F. Murray Abraham

People Who Are Fluent in Foreign Languages

Mira Sorvino (Mandarin Chinese)

Eddie Izzard (French)

Kate Beckinsale (French and Russian)

Geena Davis (Swedish)

Rachel Weisz (German)

Helena Bonham Carter (French)

Rupert Everett (French and Italian)

Alan Bennett (Russian)

Gabriel Byrne (Spanish)

Edward Norton (Japanese)

Natalie Portman (Hebrew)

Madeleine Albright (Russian)

Donna Summer (German)

Jodie Foster (French)

Ted Koppel (Russian, German and French)

Christy Turlington (Spanish)

Kirk Douglas (German)

Brigitte Nielsen (Italian and German)

Karl Lagerfeld (French and Italian)

Rosamund Pike (German and French)

Famke Janssen (German and French)

Christopher Lee (German)

Lyle Lovett (German)

Dolph Lundgren (German, French and Japanese)

Bill Paxton (German)

People Who Read Their Own Obituaries

Mark Twain

Wild Bill Hickok

Bob Hope

Elizabeth, The Queen Mother

Alfred Nobel

Bertrand Russell

P. T. Barnum

Daniel Boone

People Who Survived Plane Crashes

Clint Eastwood, Yasser Arafat, Elizabeth Taylor, Patrick Swayze, Sting, Luciano Pavarotti, Rowan Atkinson, Ted Kennedy

People Who Had a Hip Replaced

Maeve Binchy, Elizabeth Taylor, Oscar Peterson, Anita Pallenberg, Charlton Heston, John Cleese, Liza Minnelli (twice)

What a 140-Pound Person Would Weigh on Other Celestial Bodies

Pluto—7 pounds

The Moon—24 pounds

Mercury—53 pounds

Mars—53 pounds

Uranus—137 pounds

Venus—137 pounds

Saturn—151 pounds

Neptune—166 pounds

Jupiter—355 pounds

Well-Known Songs Based on Classical Music

"Lady Lynda" (The Beach Boys)—based on Bach's "Jesu, Joy of Man's Desiring"

"It's Now or Never" (Elvis Presley)—based on de Capua's "O Sole Mio"

"Stranger in Paradise" (Tony Bennett)—based on Borodin's "Polovtsian Dances"

"Could It Be Magic" (Barry Manilow)—based on Chopin's Prelude in C Major

"Joybringer" (Manfred Mann's Earth Band)—based on Holst's *The Planets*

"A Lover's Concerto" (The Toys)—based on Bach's Minuet in G

"All By Myself" (Eric Carmen)—based on Rachmaninov's Piano Concerto No. 2

"Who's Afraid of the Big Bad Wolf" (1933)—based on Johann Strauss's "Champagne Song" from *Die Fledermaus*

"Lullaby of Broadway" (1935)—based on Brahms's *Hungarian Dances* and Offenbach's "Barcarolle" from *Tales of Hoffman*

"Where Did You Get That Hat?" (1888)—based on Wagner's *Lohengrin* and *Die Meistersinger*

Well-Known Songs Based on Other Songs

"Love Me Tender" (1956)—based on George Poulton's "Aura Lee" (1861)

"El Condor Pasa" (1933)—based on a Peruvian folk song

"Waltzing Matilda" (1903)—based on Robert Tannahill's "Craigielea" (1818)

"Those Were the Days" (1968)—based on a traditional Eastern European tune

"Don't Sit Under the Apple Tree" (1942)—based on "Long Long Ago" (1833)

"It's All in the Game" (1951)—based on "Melody" by Charles Dawes (1912)

"She'll Be Comin' 'Round the Mountain (When She Comes)" (1899)—based on the hymn "When the Chariot Comes"

"Hello, Dolly" (1964)—based on "Sunflower" by Mack David (1948)

"Midnight in Moscow" (1962)—based on the Russian song "Pad Moskovniye Vietchera"

"My Sweet Lord" (1971)—based on Ronald Mack's "He's So Fine" (1962)

Famous Relatives of Olympic Competitors

Grace Kelly (her father, John Kelly, rowing, 1920, U.S.)

Jean Simmons (her father, Charles Simmons, gymnastics, 1952, U.K.)

Charlotte Rampling (her father, Godfrey Rampling, 4400 Meters, 1936, U.K.)

Prince Rainier (his son, Prince Albert, bobsled, 1988, Monaco)

Rex Harrison (his son Noel Harrison, alpine skiing, 1952, U.K.)

Andre Agassi (his father, Mike Agassi, boxing, 1948 and 1952, for Iran)

Hugh Laurie (his father, Ran Laurie, rowing—Gold Medal winner—1948, U.K.)

Lindsay Davenport (her father, Wink Davenport, volleyball, 1968, U.S.)

The Spooky Lincoln-Kennedy Coincidences

Lincoln was elected president in 1860, having been elected to Congress in 1846; Kennedy was elected president in 1960, having been elected to Congress in 1946.

Both presidents were directly concerned with civil rights for black people.

Lincoln had a secretary named Kennedy; Kennedy had a secretary named Lincoln.

Both wives had lost children while living at the White House.

Both assassinations took place on a Friday, and both presidents were warned that they might be assassinated but both refused to change their schedules.

Lincoln was shot in a theater by a man who then hid in a warehouse; Kennedy was shot from a warehouse by a man who then hid in a theater.

Kennedy was riding in a Lincoln when he was shot.

Lincoln's assassin, John Wilkes Booth, was a southerner in his twenties; Kennedy's assassin, Lee Harvey Oswald, was a southerner in his twenties.

Both assassins were known by their three names.

Booth and Oswald were both shot before they could be tried.

Lincoln was succeeded by his vice president, Andrew Johnson, who was born in 1808; Kennedy was succeeded by his vice president, Lyndon Johnson, who was born in 1908.

Lincoln and Kennedy each had 7 letters in their names; John Wilkes Booth and Lee Harvey Oswald each had 15 letters in their names; Andrew Johnson and Lyndon Johnson each had 13 letters in their names.

A month before Lincoln was assassinated, he was in Monroe, Maryland; a year before Kennedy was assassinated, he was in Marilyn Monroe.

People Who Entered Competitions to Imitate or Impersonate Themselves—and Lost

Dolly Parton

Graham Greene (entered a competition to parody his style in the *Spectator*—came in third)

Charlie Chaplin

Elvis Presley (entered an Elvis look-alike contest in a U.S. burger joint but came in third)

The Last Lines of Classic Movies

"The horror, the horror." (*Apocalypse Now*)

"Madness. Madness." (*The Bridge on the River Kwai*)

"That's right, that's right—attaboy, Clarence." (*It's a Wonderful Life*)

"I used to hate the water—I can't imagine why." (*Jaws*)

"The old man was right, only the farmers won; we lost, we'll always lose." (*The Magnificent Seven*)

"Eliza? Where the devil are my slippers?" (*My Fair Lady*)

"Why, she wouldn't even harm a fly." (*Psycho*)

"Well, Tillie, when the hell are we going to get some dinner?" (*Guess Who's Coming to Dinner?*)

"We saw her many times again, born free and living free, but to us she was always the same, our friend Elsa." (*Born Free*)

"Hello, everybody, this is Mrs. Norman Maine." (*A Star Is Born*)

"I haven't got a sensible name, Calloway." (*The Third Man*)

"Thank you, thank you, I'm glad it's off my mind at last." (*The 39 Steps*)

"Good, for a minute I thought we were in trouble." (*Butch Cassidy and the Sundance Kid*)

"All right, Mr. DeMille, I'm ready for my close-up." (*Sunset Boulevard*)

"I now pronounce you men and wives." (*Seven Brides for Seven Brothers*)

"Louis, I think this is the beginning of a beautiful friendship." (*Casablanca*)

"Oh, Aunt Em, there's no place like home." (*The Wizard of Oz*)

"The way we're swimming, old girl." (*The African Queen*)

"Mediocrities everywhere, I absolve you, I absolve you, I absolve you, I absolve you. I absolve you all." (*Amadeus*)

"Cool Hand Luke, hell, he's a natural born world-shaker." (*Cool Hand Luke*)

"I guess we all died a little in that damn war." (*The Outlaw Josey Wales*)

Famous Women Who Had Grandfathers Who Won 1954 Nobel Prizes

Olivia Newton-John (Max Born, won for Physics)

Mariel Hemingway (Ernest Hemingway, won for Literature)

Proof That Hell Is Exothermic

This was a question in a University of Washington chemistry exam: "Is Hell exothermic (gives off heat) or endothermic (absorbs heat)? Support your answer with proof." Most students wrote about Boyle's law: gas cools off when it expands and heats up when it is compressed. However, one student wrote this:

> **First,** we need to know how the mass of Hell is changing in time. So, we need to know the rate that souls are moving into Hell and the rate they are leaving. I think that we can safely assume that once a soul gets to Hell, it will not leave. Therefore, no souls are leaving. As for how many souls are entering Hell, let's look at the different religions that exist in the world today. Some of these religions state that if you are not a member of their religion, you will go to Hell. Since there are more

131

than one of these religions and since people do not belong to more than one religion, we can project that all people and all souls go to Hell. With birth and death rates as they are, we can expect the number of souls in Hell to increase exponentially. Now, we look at the rate of change of the volume in Hell because Boyle's Law states that in order for the temperature and pressure in Hell to stay the same, the volume of Hell has to expand as souls are added. This gives two possibilities: (1) If Hell is expanding at a slower rate than the rate at which souls enter Hell, then the temperature and pressure in Hell will increase until all Hell breaks loose. (2) Of course, if Hell is expanding at a rate faster than the increase of souls in Hell, then the temperature and pressure will drop until Hell freezes over. So which is it? If we accept the postulate given to me by Ms. Therese Banyan during my freshman year, that "it will be a cold night in Hell before I sleep with you," and take into account the fact that I still have not succeeded in having sexual relations with her, then (2) cannot be true and thus I am sure that Hell is exothermic.

This student received the only A.

Oscar Onlys

The only role to garner two Oscars is Vito Corleone: Marlon Brando won the Best Actor Oscar in this role for *The Godfather* (1972), while Robert De Niro won the Best Supporting Actor Oscar in the same role for *The Godfather Part II* (1974). This film is also the only sequel to win an Oscar as Best Film

The only actor to win an Oscar for less than ten minutes' work: Anthony Quinn, who was on-screen for only 9 minutes in *Lust for Life* (1956)

The only actress to win an Oscar for less than ten minutes' work: Judi Dench, who was on-screen for only eight minutes in *Shakespeare in Love* (1998)

The only Oscar to win an Oscar: Oscar Hammerstein II (Best Song: 1941 and 1945)

The only actress to win an Oscar for playing an Oscar nominee: Maggie Smith in *California Suite* (1978)

The only silent film to win Best Picture: *Wings* (1927)

The only actor to win a Best Actor Oscar when nominated alongside four previous Oscar winners: Adrien Brody for *The Pianist* (2003)

The only actor to win a Best Actor Oscar in a foreign-language film: Roberto Benigni for *Life Is Beautiful* (1998); note also that Robert De Niro's performance in *The Godfather Part II* was mostly in Italian

The only actress to win a Best Actress Oscar in a foreign language: Sophia Loren for *Two Women* (1961)

The only actress to win a Best Supporting Actress Oscar for playing the title role in a film: Vanessa Redgrave for *Julia* (1977)

The only films in which all the members of the cast have been nominated for Oscars: *Who's Afraid of Virginia Woolf?* (four cast members 1966), *Sleuth* (two cast members 1972) and *Give 'Em Hell, Harry* (one cast member 1975)

The only families in which three generations have won Oscars: The Hustons—Walter for *The Treasure of the Sierra Madre* (1948), John for *The Treasure of the Sierra Madre* and Anjelica for *Prizzi's Honor* (1985). Walter and John Huston are also the only father and son to win acting Oscars for the same film. The Coppolas—Carmine for *The Godfather Part II* (1974), his son Francis for *The Godfather Part II* (1974), and Sofia for *Lost in Translation* (2004). In addition, Francis's nephew (and Sofia's cousin) Nicolas Cage won the Best Actor Oscar for *Leaving Las Vegas* (1995)

The only mother and daughter to be nominated for Oscars in the same year: Diane Ladd and her daughter, Laura Dern, for *Rambling Rose* (1991)

The only films to win eleven Oscars: *Ben-Hur* (1959), *Titanic* (1997), and *The Lord of the Rings: The Return of the King* (2003)

The only film to win in every category for which it was nominated: *The Lord of the Rings: The Return of the King* (2003)

The only films to get eleven Oscar nominations but not a single Oscar: *The Turning Point* (1977) and *The Color Purple* (1985)

The only sisters to win Best Actress Oscars: Joan Fontaine for *Suspicion* (1941) and Olivia de Havilland for *To Each His Own* (1946). And they didn't speak to each other!

The only twins to win Oscars: Julius J. Epstein and Philip G. Epstein (with Howard Koch) for *Casablanca* (1943)

The only Oscar sold for more than half a million dollars: Vivien Leigh's for *Gone With the Wind*, which fetched $510,000 at auction in 1994

The only posthumous acting Oscar was won by Peter Finch for *Network* (1976)

The only actor to get two posthumous Oscar nominations: James Dean, for *East of Eden* (1955) and *Giant* (1956)

The only animated film nominated for Best Film: *Beauty and the Beast* (1991)

The only actress to win four Oscars: Katharine Hepburn, for *Morning Glory* (1932–33), *Guess Who's Coming to Dinner?* (1967), *The Lion in Winter* (1968) and *On Golden Pond* (1981). Jack Nicholson (two Best Actor and one Best

Supporting Actor) and Walter Brennan (all as Best Supporting Actor) hold the record for the most Oscars for actors with three.

The only Best Supporting Actor winner to perform one-armed push-ups when he received his award: Jack Palance when he won for *City Slickers* (1991)

The only father to win a Best Actor Oscar after his daughter had already won two Best Actress Oscars: Henry Fonda for *On Golden Pond*, 1981, after Jane Fonda had won for *Klute* (1971) and *Coming Home* (1978)

The only daughter of a Best Actor winner to win an Oscar for Best Supporting Actress: Angelina Jolie for *Girl, Interrupted* (1999); she is the daughter of Jon Voight, who won for *Coming Home* (1978)

The only actors to get seven acting nominations without winning a single Oscar: Peter O'Toole and Richard Burton

The only actress to get six acting nominations without winning a single Oscar: Deborah Kerr

The only two actresses to compete against each other in both the Best Actress and the Best Supporting Actress categories in the same year: Holly Hunter and Emma Thompson in 1993

The only actors to refuse Oscars: George C. Scott, *Patton* (1970) and Marlon Brando, *The Godfather* (1972)

The only actor nominated as both Best Actor and Best Supporting Actor in the same year: Al Pacino (1992)

The only octogenarian to win a Best Actress Oscar: Jessica Tandy for *Driving Miss Daisy* (1989)

The only octogenarian to win a Best Supporting Actor Oscar: George Burns for *The Sunshine Boys* (1975)

The only person to open the Oscar envelope to find his own name on the card: Irving Berlin (Best Song, "White Christmas," 1942)

The only man to be nominated for producer, director, writer and actor on the same film—twice—was Warren Beatty for *Heaven Can Wait* (1978) and *Reds* (1981)

The only film in which the Best Director Oscar was shared by two men: *West Side Story* (Robert Wise and Jerome Robbins in 1961)

The only women nominated as Best Director: Lina Wertmuller, *Seven Beauties* (1976), Jane Campion, *The Piano* (1994) and Sofia Coppola, *Lost in Translation* (2003)

The only foreign-language films nominated for Best Picture: *Grand Illusion* (1938, France), *Z* (1969, Algeria), *The Emigrants* (1972, Sweden), *Cries and Whispers* (1973, Sweden), *Il Postino* (1995, Italy), *Life Is Beautiful* (1998, Italy), *Crouching Tiger, Hidden Dragon* (2000, Taiwan)

The only actors to win consecutive Oscars: Spencer Tracy (1937 and 1938), Jason Robards (1976 and 1977) and Tom Hanks (1993 and 1994)

The only actresses to win consecutive Oscars: Luise Rainer (1936 and 1937) and Katharine Hepburn (1967 and 1968)

The only actresses to get acting nominations five years running: Bette Davis (1938–42) and Greer Garson (1941–45)

The only actors to get acting nominations four years running: Marlon Brando (1951–54) and Al Pacino (1972–75)

The only films to win Best Actor and Best Actress Oscars: *It Happened One Night* (1934), *One Flew Over the Cuckoo's Nest* (1975), *Network* (1976), *Coming Home* (1978), *On Golden Pond* (1981), *The Silence of the Lambs* (1991) and *As Good As It Gets* (1997)

The only films to win Oscars for Best Picture, Best Director, Best Actor, Best Actress and Best Screenplay: *It Happened One Night* (1934), *One Flew Over the Cuckoo's Nest* (1975) and *The Silence of the Lambs* (1991)

The only films to win three acting Oscars: *A Streetcar Named Desire* (1951) and *Network* (1976)

The only two actors to tie for Best Actor: Wallace Beery, *The Champ*, and Fredric March, *Dr. Jekyll and Mr. Hyde* (1931–32)

The only two actresses to tie for Best Actress: Katharine Hepburn, *The Lion in Winter* and Barbra Streisand, *Funny Girl* (1968)

The only actor to be nominated in both the leading and supporting categories for the same role: Barry Fitzgerald, *Going My Way* (1944)

The only people to direct themselves to acting Oscars: Laurence Olivier, *Hamlet* (1948), and Roberto Benigni, *Life Is Beautiful* (1998)

The only black actors to win Oscars: Hattie McDaniel (*Gone With the Wind*, 1939), Sidney Poitier (*Lilies of the Field*, 1963), Louis Gossett Jr. (*An Officer and a Gentleman*, 1982), Denzel Washington (*Glory*, 1989), Whoopi Goldberg (*Ghost*, 1990), Cuba Gooding Jr. (*Jerry Maguire*, 1996), Halle Berry (*Monster's Ball*, 2001), Denzel Washington (*Training Day*, 2001)

The only actor to appear in three films that were nominated for Best Picture in the same year: Thomas Mitchell (*Stagecoach, Mr. Smith Goes to Washington* and *Gone With the Wind* in 1939; he got the Best Supporting Actor Oscar for *Stagecoach*)

Note: Actors whose only Oscars have been awarded for directing: Robert Redford (1980: *Ordinary People*), Warren Beatty (1981: *Reds*), Richard Attenborough (1982: *Gandhi*), Kevin Costner (1991: *Dances with Wolves*), Mel Gibson (1995: *Braveheart*)

Famous People with Famous Godparents

Winona Ryder (Timothy Leary)

Whitney Houston (Aretha Franklin)

Jennifer Aniston (Telly Savalas)

Mia Farrow (George Cukor and Louella Parsons)

Robert Cummings (Orville Wright)

Drew Barrymore (Steven Spielberg)

Bridget Fonda (Larry Hagman)

Angelina Jolie (Jacqueline Bisset)

The World's Greatest Urban Myth

Good Luck, Mr. Gorsky: On July 20, 1969, Neil Armstrong, commander of *Apollo 11*, was the first person to set foot on the moon. His first words—"That's one small step for a man, one giant leap for mankind"—were heard by millions. He then said, "Good luck, Mr. Gorsky." People at NASA thought he was talking about a Soviet cosmonaut, but it turned out there was no Gorsky in the Russian space program. Over the years Armstrong was frequently asked what he had meant by "Good luck, Mr. Gorsky," but he always refused to answer for fear of offending the man.

After Mr. Gorsky died, Neil Armstrong finally felt able to tell the story. When he was a kid playing in his backyard, he once had to fetch his ball from the neighbors' yard. As he dashed in, he overheard his neighbor, Mrs. Gorsky, shouting at Mr. Gorsky, "Sex! You want sex? You'll get sex when the kid next door walks on the moon!"

Alas, not only is the story untrue, but Neil Armstrong never even uttered the words "Good luck, Mr. Gorsky." This story is an urban myth that has gathered currency on the Internet. It's a prime example of the old saw that a lie can be halfway around the world before the truth has even got its boots on.

Wonderfully Named Characters from the World of P. G. Wodehouse's Bertie Wooster

Barmy Fotheringay-Phipps, Stilton Cheesewright, Pongo Twistleton-Twistleton, Gussie Fink-Nottle, Biscuit Biskerton, Stiffy Stiffham, Catsmeat Potter-Pirbright, Dogface Rainsby, Oofy Prosser, Freddie Fitch-Fitch

People Who Guested on the *Batman* TV Series

Shelley Winters (Ma Parker)

Ethel Merman (Lola Lasagne)

Tallulah Bankhead (Mrs. Max Black)

Anne Baxter (Olga, Queen of the Cossacks)

Bruce Lee (Kato)

Glynis Johns (Lady Penelope Peasoup)

Jock Mahoney (Leo, one of Catwoman's accomplices)

James Brolin (Ralph Staphylococcus)

Michael Rennie (The Sandman)

George Sanders (Mr. Freeze)

Zsa Zsa Gabor (Minerva)

Roddy McDowall (The Bookworm)

Art Carney (The Archer)

Joan Collins (The Siren)

Vincent Price (Egghead)

Liberace (Chandell)

Cliff Robertson (Shame)

Eartha Kitt (Catwoman)

Julie Newmar (Catwoman)

Lee Meriwether (Catwoman)

Edward G. Robinson (cameo role)

George Raft (cameo role)

Phyllis Diller (cameo role)

Jerry Lewis (cameo role)

Gypsy Rose Lee (cameo role)

Rob Reiner (cameo role)

Sammy Davis Jr. (cameo role)

Note: Robert F. Kennedy, Frank Sinatra, Jose Ferrer, Yul Brynner, Elizabeth Taylor, Gregory Peck, Mae West, Gloria Swanson and Cary Grant all wanted to appear, but no parts could be found for them.

How to Say "Beer" in Different Languages

cerveza (Spanish)

cerveja (Portuguese)

sor (Hungarian)

bière (French)

Bier (German)

bjór (Icelandic)

pombe (Swahili)

pivo (Russian)

öl (Swedish)

øl (Danish and Norwegian)

olut (Finnish)

bira (Turkish)

bir (Indonesian)

bere (Romanian)

birra (Italian)

beera (Greek)

fermentum/cervisia (Latin)

Famous People Born on the Very Same Day As Other Famous People Died

Davy Crockett and Frederick the Great—8/17/1786

Billie Jean King and Lorenz Hart—11/22/43

Laura Dern and Billy Rose—2/10/66

Donald Trump and John Logie Baird—6/14/46

famous people born on the very same day as other famous people died

Bryan Ferry and Béla Bartók—9/26/45

Kevin Costner and George Morrow—1/18/55

Kian Egan and Sir Alfred Hitchcock—4/29/80

Rutger Hauer and Edvard Munch—1/23/44

Jason Donovan and Helen Keller—6/1/68

Yoko Ono and Gentleman Jim Corbett—2/18/33

Adam Ant and Henri Matisse—11/3/54

Michael Stipe and Albert Camus—1/4/60

Frank Zappa and F. Scott Fitzgerald—12/21/40

Che Guevara and Emmeline Pankhurst—6/14/28

Johnny Rotten and A. A. Milne—1/31/56

Julia Ormond and T. S. Eliot—1/4/65

Billy Ocean and George Orwell—1/21/50

Germaine Greer and W. B. Yeats—1/29/39

Mickey Rourke and Hilaire Belloc—7/16/53

Patrick Ewing and Marilyn Monroe—8/5/62

Adam Sandler and Hendrik Verwoerd—9/6/66

James Gandolfini and Dag Hammarskjöld—9/18/61

Janeane Garofalo and Harpo Marx—9/28/64

Richard Carpenter and Hermann Göring—10/15/46

Winona Ryder and Duane Allman—10/29/71

k. d. lang and James Thurber—11/2/61

Robert F. Kennedy and Queen Alexandra—11/20/25

David Mamet and Ernst Lubitsch—11/30/47

Comic-Book Superheroes and Their Everyday Identities

Spiderman (Peter Parker)

Superman (Clark Kent)

Batman (Bruce Wayne)

Robin (Dick Grayson)

The Green Hornet (Britt Reid)

Supergirl (Linda Lee Danvers)

Batgirl (Babs Gordon)

The Incredible Hulk (Bruce Banner)

Captain Marvel (Billy Batson)

Wonder Woman (Diana Prince)

Women Who Had Songs Written for Them

Marilyn Monroe—"Candle in the Wind" (Elton John/Bernie Taupin)

Elizabeth Taylor—"Emotionally Yours" (Bob Dylan)

Christie Brinkley—"Uptown Girl" (Billy Joel)

Joni Mitchell—"Our House" (Graham Nash)

Billie Jean King—"Philadelphia Freedom" (Elton John/Bernie Taupin)

Joan Baez—"It Ain't Me, Babe" (Bob Dylan)

Kylie Minogue—"Suicide Blonde" (Michael Hutchence)

Marianne Faithfull—"Wild Horses" (Mick Jagger)

Geri Halliwell—"Eternity" (Robbie Williams)

Patti Boyd—"Layla" (Eric Clapton)

Rita Coolidge—"Delta Lady" (Leon Russell)

Judy Collins—"Suite: Judy Blue Eyes" (Stephen Stills)

Great Country and Western Titles

"You're the Reason Our Kids Are Ugly" (Loretta Lynn)

"I Cheated Me Right Out of You" (Moe Bandy)

"You're Out Doing What I'm Here Doing Without" (Gene Watson)

"The Lord Knows I'm Drinkin'" (Cal Smith)

"She Got the Goldmine (I Got the Shaft)" (Jerry Reed)

"Now I Lay Me Down to Cheat" (David Allan Coe)

"You Just Hurt My Last Feeling" (Sammi Smith)

"She's Actin' Single (I'm Drinkin' Doubles)" (Gary Stewart)

"I'm Gonna Hire a Wino to Decorate Our Home" (David Frizzell)

"Divorce Me C.O.D." (Merle Travis)

"Heaven's Just a Sin Away" (The Kendells)

"I Forgot More Than You'll Ever Know" (The Davis Sisters)

"I'm the Only Hell (Mama Ever Raised)" (Johnny Paycheck)

Some More Actual Song Titles

"I'd Rather Be a Lobster Than a Wiseguy" (Edward Madden and Theodore F. Morse, 1907)

"(Potatoes Are Cheaper—Tomatoes Are Cheaper) Now's the Time to Fall in Love" (Al Lewis and Al Sherman, 1931)

"Hey Young Fella! (Close Your Old Umbrella)" (Dorothy Fields and Jimmy McHugh, 1933)

"Caldonia (What Makes Your Big Head So Hard?)" (Fleecie Moore, 1946)

"Aunt Jemima and Your Uncle Cream of Wheat" (Johnny Mercer and Rube Bloom, 1936)

"Come After Breakfast, Bring 'Long Your Lunch and Leave 'Fore Supper Time" (J. Tim Bryman, Chris Smith and James Henry Burris, 1909)

"I Love to Dunk a Hunk of Sponge Cake" (Clarence Gaskill, 1928)

"Who Ate Napoleons with Josephine When Bonaparte Was Away?" (Alfred Bryan and E. Ray Gotz, 1920)

"All the Quakers Are Shoulder Shakers Down in Quaker Town" (Bert Kalmar, Edgar Leslie and Pete Wendling, 1919)

Famous People Who Are Vegans

William Shatner, Alicia Silverstone, Woody Harrelson, Joaquin Phoenix, Moby, Bryan Adams, Carl Lewis, Uri Geller, k. d. lang, Sinéad O'Connor, Brandy Norwood, Casey Affleck, Linda Blair, Julia Stiles

Some Deadly Australian Creatures

The blue-ringed octopus—one bite or squirt causes immediate paralysis and death in minutes.

The "sea wasp" or box jellyfish—human survival rate almost zero; time from its transparent sting to death, 4 minutes.

The Taipan snake is 180 times more venomous than the king cobra—one bite can kill 12,000 guinea pigs, and a human within 3 seconds.

The tiger snake—death takes 12 hours. Antidote available but must be used within 30 minutes of bite; single snake has enough venom to kill 118 sheep.

The funnel-web spider—tree dweller, one of the most dangerous spiders in the world; kills humans within 15 minutes.

Conus textile shells—underwater sea creature with 21 darts, each of which has enough poison to kill 300 people; death in minutes.

Irukandji jellyfish—deadly transparent sea creature with poisonous tentacles; sting causes heart attacks in humans, leaving swimmers to drown.

The saltwater crocodile—kills 2,000 people a year because it is fast in and out of water; it can outrun a galloping horse and kills in seconds.

The great white shark—the most dangerous of the many sharks in Aussie waters; kills in seconds with just one snap of its awesome teeth.

Red-backed spider—the female is the deadly variety, and it kills in a few minutes, but deaths have ceased since an antidote was found.

Pairs of Famous People Who Died on the Same Day

Freddie Mercury (rock star) and Klaus Kinski (actor)—11/24/91

Maria Callas (opera singer) and Marc Bolan (rock star)— 9/16/77

Fred Perry (tennis player) and Donald Pleasence (actor)—2/2/95

G. K. Chesterton (writer) and Maxim Gorky (writer)—6/14/36

Rudolf Nureyev (ballet dancer) and Dizzy Gillespie (jazz musician)— 1/6/93

P. G. Wodehouse (writer) and Julian Huxley (scientist)—2/14/75

Orson Welles (film director and actor) and Yul Brynner (actor)—10/10/85

Cecil Day-Lewis (poet) and Margaret Rutherford (actress)—5/22/72

Orville Wright (aviation pioneer) and Mohandas Gandhi (Indian leader)—1/30/48

David Niven (actor and author) and Raymond Massey (actor)—7/29/83

Anthony Eden (former British prime minister) and Peter Finch (actor)—1/14/77

Bernard Miles (actor and producer) and Peggy Ashcroft (actress)—6/14/91

Sammy Davis Jr. (entertainer) and Jim Henson (the man behind the Muppets)—5/16/90

River Phoenix (actor) and Federico Fellini (film director)—10/31/93

Earl Spencer (Princess Diana's father) and Paul Henreid (actor)—3/29/92

John F. Kennedy (U.S. president) and Aldous Huxley (writer)—11/22/63

General Leopoldo Galtieri (former Argentinian dictator) and Maurice Gibb (musician)—1/12/2003

John Lee Hooker (blues legend) and Carroll O'Connor (actor)—6/21/01

Christiaan Barnard (pioneering heart surgeon) and Troy Donahue (actor)—9/2/01

Men Who Were the Seventh Sons of Seventh Sons

Glen Campbell

Perry Como

The Working Titles of Classic Television Programs

The Waltons: *Spencer's Mountain*

Happy Days: *New Family in Town*

The Flintstones: *The Flagstones*

Beverly Hills 90210: *The Class of Beverly Hills*

Diff'rent Strokes: *45 Minutes from Harlem*

Falcon Crest: *The Vintage Years*

The Man from U.N.C.L.E.: *Mr. Solo*

The Partridge Family: *Family Business*

Seinfeld: *The Seinfeld Chronicles*

Charlie's Angels: *The Alley Cats*

Tribute Bands

Led Zeppelin: Whole Lotta Led

The Beatles: The Bootleg Beatles

The Rolling Stones: The Counterfeit Stones

Radiohead: No Surprises

U2: The Joshua Trio

Oasis: Noasis

The Stranglers: No More Heroes

The Eagles: The Illegal Eagles

The Corrs: The Coors

The Beautiful South: The Beautiful Southmartins

Queen: Royal Family

Steely Dan: Nearly Dan

Black Sabbath: Sabbra Cadabra

The Stranglers: The Men in Black

Erasure: Erasured

The Doors: The Australian Doors

Abba: Bjorn Again

Extraordinary Bequests

In 1987, Bob Fosse, the choreographer and film director (he won an Oscar for *Cabaret*), left $378.79 to each of 66 people to "go out and have dinner on me"; these included Liza Minnelli, Janet Leigh, Elia Kazan, Dustin Hoffman, Melanie Griffith, Neil Simon, Ben Gazzara, Jessica Lange and Roy Scheider.

In 1974, Philip Grundy, a British dentist, left his dental nurse $271,500 on condition that she didn't wear any makeup or jewelry or go out with men for five years.

In 1955, Juan Potomachi, an Argentinian, left more than $37,500 to the local theater on the condition that they used his skull when performing *Hamlet*.

In 1765, John Hart left his brother a gun and a bullet "in the hope that he will put the same through his head when the money is spent."

An unnamed Irishman left $2,250 in his will to the British Department of Health and Social Security (as it then was called) to repay the money he had received while on the dole.

In 1950, George Bernard Shaw left a considerable portion of his estate for the purpose of replacing the standard English alphabet of twenty-six letters with a more efficient alphabet of at least forty letters—it was never achieved.

The British dramatist Richard Brinsley Sheridan told his son that he was cutting him out of his will with just a shilling. His son's reaction was, "I'm sorry to hear that, sir. You don't happen to have the shilling about you now, do you?"

In 1856, Heinrich Heine, the German poet, left everything to his wife on the condition that she remarried "so that there will be at least one man to regret my death."

An unnamed Scotsman bequeathed each of his two daughters her weight in one-pound notes. The elder, slimmer daughter received £51,200 (now the equivalent of $76,800), while her younger, fatter sister got £57,433 ($86,150).

The longest will in the world was one drawn up for Frederica Cook, an American woman—when it was probated at London's Somerset House in 1925, it consisted of four bound volumes totaling 95,940 words. Amazingly, she didn't have all that much to leave.

The shortest valid British will—which was contested but eventually passed after the 1906 case *Thorne* v. *Dickens*—consisted of three words: "All for mother." What caused the confusion was that the testator didn't mean his mother but his wife.

William Shakespeare bequeathed to his wife, Anne, "my second best bed." This has been interpreted as a snub. In fact, his "second best bed" was probably the one most used by the two of them, and it was therefore a sentimental gesture. His best bed went to the male heirs of his elder daughter.

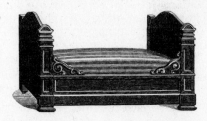

In 1937, F. Scott Fitzgerald drew up a will in which he specified "a funeral and burial in keeping with my station in life." Three years later, just before his death, a much poorer Fitzgerald amended this provision to read "cheapest funeral . . . without undue ostentation or unnecessary expense"—his funeral cost precisely $613.25.

In 1975, Edward Horley, a former mayor of Altrincham, UK, instructed his solicitors to buy a lemon, cut it in two and send one half to the income-tax inspectorate and the other half to the tax collector with the message "Now squeeze this."

Charles Millar, a straitlaced Canadian lawyer who died in 1928 at the age of seventy-three, had a bizarre sense of humor. He wondered how much people would do in the pursuit of money. To a preacher and a judge, who were both against gambling, he left shares in a racetrack that would make both men automatic members of a horse-racing club. Both accepted. To a group of ministers who were antialcohol, Millar left $50,000 worth of shares in a brewery—they all accepted bar one. To three acquaintances who loathed each other, Millar bequeathed a holiday home in Jamaica that they were obliged to share—which they did. Most controversially, Millar bequeathed more than $500,000 to the Toronto woman who "has given birth to the greatest number of children at the expiration of ten years from my death." Millar's relatives tried—but failed—to overturn the will and, ten years later, four women who had each had nine children in the ten years shared the money.

A wealthy American banker left a codicil in his will cutting out two members of his family: "To my wife and her lover, I leave the knowledge I wasn't the fool she thought I was. To my son I leave the pleasure of earning a living. For twenty-five years he thought the pleasure was mine."

In 1997, Robert Brett, a Californian who wasn't allowed to smoke at home, left his entire fortune to his wife, provided that she smoked four cigars a day for the rest of her life.

Anagrams

"To be or not to be: that is the question: / Whether tis nobler in the mind to suffer / The slings and arrows of outrageous fortune" is an anagram of "In one of the Bard's best-thought-of tragedies, our insistent hero, Hamlet, queries on two fronts about how life turns rotten."

Neil Armstrong's "That's one small step for a man, one giant leap for mankind" is an anagram of "Thin man ran; makes a large stride, left planet, pins flag on moon! On to Mars!"

Eric Clapton (NARCOLEPTIC) and Britney Spears (PRESBYTERIANS) both have names that can be anagrammatized into single words.

WORKABLE CARAMEL LIPS—Camilla Parker Bowles

LARGE FAT NOISE—Gloria Estefan

NOT ARENA KING—Ronan Keating

GROAN MADLY—Gary Oldman

HER ILLEGAL CHARM SALE—Sarah Michelle Gellar

MOANS LYRIC—Carly Simon

BLAME, COMPLAIN—Naomi Campbell

I'M AS CHEAP BENEATH—Stephanie Beacham

DOCILE OR PARANOID—Leonardo DiCaprio

NO NEAR SHOTS—Sharon Stone

DO "ANNIE" TAKE—Diane Keaton

AMERICAN YELLS "HI!"—Shirley Maclaine

NO ALIENS, DARLING—Gillian Anderson

I WARM BILLIONS—Robin Williams

REVIEW AGONY SURE—Sigourney Weaver

OLD WEST ACTION—Clint Eastwood

VALUES SLIM WIN—Venus Williams

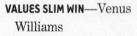

ANORAK'S IN TOWN—Rowan Atkinson

NATIVE NODDY—Danny DeVito

CAP STAR TREK WIT—Patrick Stewart

PAY MR. CLEAN-CUT—Paul McCartney

BEST PG—NEVER LIES—Steven Spielberg

GOD, I DO COMPLAIN—Plácido Domingo

GIRLIE LAW HELL—Geri Halliwell

DIET? TREMBLE!—Bette Midler

BLOB RECREATION—Robbie Coltrane

COOL OGRE IMMINENT—Colin Montgomerie

IN TONE—WHY SHOUT?—Whitney Houston

ERROR ON BIDET—Robert De Niro

EVIL LASS IN EROTICA—Alicia Silverstone

NO, I DECLINE—Céline Dion

HERE IS SHINY CD—Chrissie Hynde

MARK A BITCH VOICE—Victoria Beckham (or **BRAVO! I'M ACE THICK**)

MORMON IDEAS—Marie Osmond

BURSTING PRESENCE—Bruce Springsteen

EACH TIMELY FALL—Michael Flatley

BEGS HUGE ROW—George W. Bush

SLICE SO MEAN—Monica Seles

GRASS AN AIDE—Andre Agassi

BORN INSANE? NO!—Anne Robinson

ASCEND IN PARIS—Princess Diana

SLOVENLY STEEL STAR—Sylvester Stallone

JUST A BROILER—Julia Roberts

HURRAH TO BORED ACTING!—Richard Attenborough

RIGHT FEE IN A FILM—Melanie Griffith

NO REAL CHARM BENEATH—Helena Bonham Carter

RUDE? I'M HYPED!—Eddie Murphy

Adult Actors Who Played Children

Richard Attenborough (*The Guinea Pig*)

Ginger Rogers (*The Major and the Minor*)

Joan Fontaine (*Letter from an Unknown Woman*)

Cary Grant (*Monkey Business*)

Bette Davis (*Payment on Demand*)

How Rock Groups Got Their Names

ABBA From the initials of the four members of the band: Agnetha, Björn, Benny and Anni-Frid. Anni-Frid, however, is now known as Frida. This means that the ABBA Fan Club is now really the ABBF Fan Club.

Bad Company The band took its name from the title of a 1972 Jeff Bridges film.

The Beatles All The Beatles were fans of Buddy Holly and the Crickets, and so John decided to call his band the Beetles. Then he changed it to "Beatles" as they were a beat band.

Deacon Blue From a song by Steely Dan, "Deacon Blues."

Dire Straits A friend, noting the band's perilous financial position, suggested the name.

The Doobie Brothers "Doobie" was American slang for a marijuana joint.

The Doors Taken from a line written by Aldous Huxley: "All the other chemical Doors in the Wall are labeled Dope. . . ."

Duran Duran From the name of the villain—played by Milo O'Shea—in the Jane Fonda film *Barbarella*.

Eurythmics Named after an early-twentieth-century form of dance and mime ("Eurhythmics") based on Greek methods of teaching children music through movement.

Foo Fighters Took their name from the nickname that Allied forces in World War II gave to unidentified glowing spheres.

Iron Maiden After a medieval torture device (consisting of a metal form with spikes on the inside).

Judas Priest Taken from the title of the Bob Dylan song "The Ballad of Frankie Lee and Judas Priest."

Led Zeppelin From the Keith Moon (then drummer with the Who) line—which he often used—"That went down like a lead zeppelin." The band later dropped the *a* in *lead*.

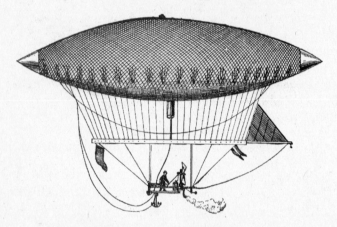

Level 42 Took their name from *The Hitchhiker's Guide to the Galaxy* by Douglas Adams, in which the number 42 is the answer to the "meaning of life."

The Lovin' Spoonful From the words of a Mississippi John Hurt song, "Coffee Blues"; this is bluesmen's slang for what a man gives a woman during sex.

Lynyrd Skynyrd Named themselves after Leonard Skinner, a disliked gym teacher at their high school.

Oasis The name came from a sports center in Swindon.

Pink Floyd They named themselves after legendary bluesmen Pink Anderson and Floyd Council.

The Pogues Short for the Gaelic *pogue mahone*, which means "kiss my ass."

Prefab Sprout As a child, singer Paddy McAloon had misheard the words "pepper sprout" in a Nancy Sinatra song as "prefab sprout," and that's the name he always wanted to give his band.

The Pretenders After the Sam Cooke song "The Great Pretender."

Radiohead From the Talking Heads song "Radiohead."

The Righteous Brothers When the duo performed at black clubs, they were praised with the words "That's righteous, brother."

The Rolling Stones Named themselves after a Muddy Waters song, "Rollin' Stones."

The Searchers Named themselves after the John Ford classic that starred John Wayne and Natalie Wood.

Simple Minds From the lyrics of the David Bowie song "Jean Genie."

Soft Machine Took their name from a novel by William Burroughs (see also Steely Dan).

Steely Dan From the William Burroughs novel *Naked Lunch*, in which Steely Dan was a steam-powered dildo.

Super Furry Animals A friend gave them a T-shirt bearing the words "Super Furry Animals," and they decided to adopt the name for their group.

The Teardrop Explodes Taken from a caption in a comic book.

Tears for Fears From the methods (in primal scream therapy) used by the psychiatrist Arthur Janov.

Three Dog Night From the Australian slang for a freezing night (in the outback, a man would need to sleep with one dog to keep warm on a cold night, two dogs on a very cold night and three dogs on the coldest night).

The Velvet Underground Taken from the title of a pornographic book about sadomasochism.

> **Wet Wet Wet** Took their name from words in a Scritti Politti song, "Getting, Having and Holding."

ZZ Top Billy Gibbons, the band's vocalist, was inspired by the Z beams on a pair of open hayloft doors.

Extraordinary Executions and Nonexecutions

In Britain in the eighteenth and nineteenth centuries, people—including children—were hanged for incredibly trivial offenses. In 1819, Thomas Wildish was hanged for stealing letters; in 1750, Benjamin Beckonfield was hanged for the theft of a hat; in 1833, an unnamed nine-year-old boy was hanged for stealing a penny's worth of paint from a shop; in 1782, a fourteen-year-old girl was hanged for being found in the company of Gypsies.

> **In 1948, the Briton William John Gray** was sentenced to hang for the murder of his wife. However, he was reprieved after medical examiners ruled that hanging would cause him too much pain. This was based on the extent of injuries to his jaw. It was explained that if he were hanged, the noose wouldn't dislocate his neck and that either he would die of strangulation or he would be decapitated altogether, as his injured jawbone was too weak to hold the rope around his neck.

In 1679, Messrs. Green, Berry and Hill were hanged at Tyburn for a murder they committed on . . . Greenberry Hill.

On August 16, 1264, at precisely nine o'clock in the morning, Inetta de Balsham was hanged. The king's messenger arrived a few seconds later with a reprieve. The hangman ran up the stairs and cut the rope with a sword. The victim's face had already turned blue, but she survived.

Similarly, in 1705, John Smith was hanged for burglary at Tyburn Tree. After he had been hanging for fifteen minutes, a reprieve arrived and he was cut down. He was revived and managed to recover. As a result of his experience, he became known as John "Half-Hanged" Smith.

In 1736, Thomas Reynolds was hanged for robbery at Tyburn Hill. He was cut down and placed in a coffin. However, as the hangman's assistant was nailing down the coffin lid, the lid was pushed away and the assistant's arm was grabbed from within. Reynolds was then taken out of the coffin and to a nearby house, where he vomited three pints of blood and died.

In 1650, charged with the murder of her newborn baby (a crime that only ceased to be a capital offense in 1922), Ann Green was hanged at Oxford Gaol. After an hour, she was cut down but was seen to be twitching. One person jumped on her stomach, and a soldier struck her on the head with his musket. Her body was then passed on to a professor of anatomy, who was preparing to cut her open when he heard a noise from her throat. She was put into a warm bed, and her breathing restarted. By the next day, she was almost fully recovered, and she was eventually pardoned.

On February 23, 1885, John Lee was due to be hanged at Exeter Gaol for the murder of his employer (on thin circumstantial evidence). However, after the hangman put the noose around his neck, the scaffold's drop wouldn't respond to the lever. Lee was returned to his cell while the hangman tested the drop with weights until it worked perfectly. A second attempt was made, but once again the drop didn't work. When Lee stood on the scaffold for the third time, it again proved impossible. Lee was returned to his cell and later given a reprieve by the home secretary. He became famous as "The Man They Couldn't Hang."

Being a hangman was no insurance against being hanged. Four English hangmen were hanged: Cratwell in 1538 for robbing a booth at St. Bartholomew's Fair, Stump-leg in 1558 for thieving, Pascha Rose in 1686 for housebreaking and theft and John Price in 1718 for murdering an old woman.

> **Postscript:** Albert Pierrepoint was Britain's last executioner. He hanged more than four hundred people. After his retirement, he campaigned for abolition, saying, "I do not now believe that any of the hundreds of executions I carried out have in any way acted as a deterrent against future murder. Capital punishment, in my view, achieved nothing except revenge."

People and Their Tattoos

Anna Kournikova: a sun on her bottom

Kelly Osbourne: small heart on her hip and a small etching on the back of her neck

Colin Farrell: ex-wife Amelia Warner's name on his finger and CARPE DIEM on his forearm

Sarah Michelle Gellar: Chinese character for integrity on her lower back

Robbie Williams: lion on his shoulder with BORN TO BE MILD underneath; on his other arm he has a Maori design. Also has the Alcoholics Anonymous Serenity Prayer tattooed on his arm, but has replaced the word GOD with ELVIS.

Eminem: SLIT ME on his wrists; the name of his wife, Kim, on his stomach with a tombstone and the inscription ROT IN FLAMES; an Indian tribal tattoo on his forearm

Charlize Theron: fish—her mother has a matching tattoo

Jude Law: SEXY SADIE on his arm

Angelina Jolie: a tattoo on her belly that reads QUOD ME NUTRIT ME DESTRUIT—"What feeds me destroys me"

Roseanne: pink rose on left foot; ex-husband Tom Arnold's name on shoulder and bottom, now replaced with flowers and fairies

Gerard Depardieu: star on arm

Mel C: Celtic band on arm, huge phoenix on back and Chinese dragon running the length of her calf

Cher: flower on bottom

Vanilla Ice: leaf on stomach

Drew Barrymore: butterfly and flower sprig on bottom

Ringo Starr: half moon on arm

Madonna: MP—standing for "Madonna's Property"—and Marilyn Monroe's face on bottom

Julia Roberts: red heart with a Chinese character meaning "strength of heart" on shoulder

Sean Connery: SCOTLAND FOREVER and MUM AND DAD on arms

Björk: Icelandic rune on shoulder

Melanie Griffith: pear on bottom

Geri Halliwell: sundial design on top of back and jaguar farther down

Marianne Faithfull: bird on hand

Chrissie Hynde: dolphin on arm

Helen Mirren: pair of crosses on hand

George Shultz: tiger on bottom

Princess Stephanie of Monaco: dragon on hip

Rachel Williams: arrow on bottom

Joan Baez: flower on back

Glen Campbell: dagger on arm

Kelly McGillis: red rose on ankle

Christy Turlington: heart shape on ankle

Whoopi Goldberg: Woodstock on breast

Natasha Henstridge: intertwined male and female symbols on her coccyx; bearded lion with crown— her star sign is Leo—on her bottom

Kelis: a giant orchid on her bottom

Ewan McGregor: heart and dagger on his right shoulder

Rachel Hunter: bee logo for her production company, Bee Knees, on her lower back

Elijah Wood: elvish symbol on his hip

Famous Novels Originally Rejected by Publishers

The Time Machine (H. G. Wells)

The Mysterious Affair at Styles (Agatha Christie)

Harry Potter and the Philosopher's Stone (J. K. Rowling)

The Razor's Edge (W. Somerset Maugham)

The Good Earth (Pearl Buck)

The Picture of Dorian Gray (Oscar Wilde)

Moby-Dick (Herman Melville)

The Naked and the Dead (Norman Mailer)

Northanger Abbey (Jane Austen)

The Ginger Man (J. P. Donleavy)

Catch-22 (Joseph Heller)

The Wind in the Willows (Kenneth Grahame)

A Time to Kill (John Grisham)

The Rainbow (D. H. Lawrence)

The Spy Who Came in from the Cold (John Le Carré)

Animal Farm (George Orwell)

Tess of the D'Urbervilles (Thomas Hardy)

Lord of the Flies (William Golding)

Great Novels and Their Original Titles

Lady Chatterley's Lover (D. H. Lawrence): *Tenderness*

Roots (Alex Haley): *Before This Anger*

The Postman Always Rings Twice (James M. Cain): *Bar-B-Q*

The Mill on the Floss (George Eliot): *Sister Maggie*

Portnoy's Complaint (Philip Roth): *A Jewish Patient Begins His Analysis*

A Portrait of the Artist As a Young Man (James Joyce): *Stephen Hero*

East of Eden (John Steinbeck): *The Salinas Valley*

The Time Machine (H. G. Wells): *The Chronic Argonauts*

Valley of the Dolls (Jacqueline Susann): *They Don't Build Statues to Businessmen*

Catch-22 (Joseph Heller): *Catch-18*

Treasure Island (Robert Louis Stevenson): *The Sea-Cook*

Jaws (Peter Benchley): *The Summer of the Shark*

War and Peace (Leo Tolstoy): *All's Well That Ends Well*

Moby-Dick (Herman Melville): *The Whale*

Of Mice and Men (John Steinbeck): *Something That Happened*

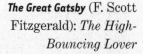

The Great Gatsby (F. Scott Fitzgerald): *The High-Bouncing Lover*

Gone With the Wind (Margaret Mitchell): *Ba! Ba! Black Sheep*

Frankenstein (Mary Shelley): *Prometheus Unchained*

Book Titles and Their Literary Origins

From Here to Eternity (James Jones): taken from Rudyard Kipling's "Gentlemen-Rankers"

Brave New World (Aldous Huxley): taken from William Shakespeare's *The Tempest upon Emergent Occasions*

For Whom the Bell Tolls (Ernest Hemingway): taken from John Donne's *Devotions*

The Moon's a Balloon (David Niven): taken from e.e. cummings's "& N &"

Now, Voyager (Olive Higgins Prouty): taken from Walt Whitman's *Leaves of Grass*

Under the Greenwood Tree (Thomas Hardy): taken from William Shakespeare's *As You Like It*

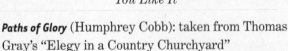

Paths of Glory (Humphrey Cobb): taken from Thomas Gray's "Elegy in a Country Churchyard"

Of Mice and Men (John Steinbeck): taken from Robert Burns's "To a Mouse"

A Confederacy of Dunces (John Kennedy Toole): taken from Jonathan Swift's "Thoughts on Various Subjects"

Gone With the Wind (Margaret Mitchell): taken from Ernest Dowson's "Cynara"

The Grapes of Wrath (John Steinbeck): taken from Julia Ward Howe's "The Battle Hymn of the Republic"

Tender Is the Night (F. Scott Fitzgerald): taken from John Keats's "Ode to a Nightingale"

The Dogs of War (Frederick Forsyth): taken from William Shakespeare's *Julius Caesar*

Extraordinary Events That (Almost) Defy Explanation

Double Proof A pair of identical American twin boys were separated at birth in 1940 and adopted by different people who didn't know each other. Each boy was named James, each boy married a woman named Linda, had a son named James Alan and was then divorced. When they eventually met up at the age of thirty-nine, they found that their hobbies, experiences and tastes had been and were remarkably similar.

Baby Luck Some coincidences are just too extraordinary. In 1975 in Detroit, a baby fell out of a building fourteen stories up. Fortunately, it landed on a man named Joseph Figlock and so survived. A year later, another baby fell from the same building and survived by falling on . . . Joseph Figlock.

Live Mushrooms A nun at a convent in Clwyd tried but failed to grow mushrooms in the convent grounds. She died at the age of seventy-nine in 1986, and a decent crop of mushrooms has grown on her grave every autumn since. Nowhere else in the convent do mushrooms grow.

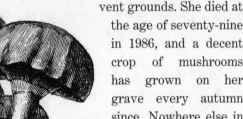

Spontaneous Combustion In 1938, Phyllis Newcombe, twenty-two, combusted spontaneously at a dance hall during a waltz. Many people witnessed this unexplained phenomenon, which has parallels with the combustion of a British pensioner, Euphemia Johnson, who died after suddenly bursting into fire during her afternoon tea.

A Golden Sheep In 1984, a Greek Orthodox priest was cooking a sheep's head when he discovered that the sheep had a jaw composed of fourteen-karat gold (worth some $6,000). The sheep had come from a herd owned by the priest's own brother-in-law, and he couldn't come up with any plausible explanation—nor could the Greek ministry of agriculture when they looked into the case.

Let It Rain In 1986, American judge Samuel King was annoyed that some jurors were absent from his Californian court because of heavy rain, so he issued a decree: "I hereby order that it cease raining by Tuesday." California suffered a five-year drought. So in 1991 the judge decreed, "Rain shall fall in California beginning February 27." Later that day, California had its heaviest rainfall in a decade.

Dead Again In Bermuda, two brothers were killed precisely one year apart at the age of seventeen by the same taxi driver carrying the same passenger on the same street. The two boys had each been riding the same moped.

A Time to Die It is said that when a person dies, his or her spouse often dies soon afterward, but this is exceptional. Charles Davies died at three in the morning at his sister's house in Leicester. When his sister phoned his home in Leeds to tell his wife, she discovered that Charles's wife had also just died . . . at three in the morning.

Some Things to Know About U.S. Presidents

Herbert Hoover (1929–33) and his wife both spoke fluent Chinese. Hoover was also the first president to have a telephone on his desk in the White House.

When Calvin Coolidge (1923–29) was being driven in a car, he would always insist that the driver didn't exceed sixteen miles per hour.

Andrew Jackson (1829–37) once killed a man in a duel because he had insulted his wife.

Ulysses S. Grant (1869–77) was tone deaf and once said, "I only know two tunes. One of them is 'Yankee Doodle,' and the other isn't."

George Washington (1789–97) had wooden false teeth.

James Garfield (1881) could write in Greek with one hand while simultaneously writing in Latin with the other.

At 340 pounds William Howard Taft (1909–13) was the heaviest president and once had the misfortune of getting stuck in the White House bathtub. At just over 100 pounds, James Madison (1809–17) was the lightest president.

Jimmy Carter (1977–81) developed the knack of speed reading and was once tested and found to have 95 percent comprehension at a reading rate of 2,000 words a minute.

Ronald Reagan (1981–89) was the first—and so far only—president to have been divorced.

George Bush (1989–93), a chubby toddler, was nicknamed "Fatty McGee McGaw" by his father.

James Buchanan (1857–61) was the first—and so far only—bachelor to become president. He also suffered from an unfortunate nervous twitch that caused his head to jerk frequently.

> **When he was young, Rutherford Hayes** (1877–81) suffered from a strange phobia: the fear of going insane.

The first president to leave the United States while in office was Theodore Roosevelt (1901–09), in 1906, when he visited the Panama Canal zone. He was also the first and only president to be a master of jujitsu.

> **Calvin Coolidge** (1923–29) was famous for being a man of few words. At a White House dinner, a female guest told him that her father had bet her she wouldn't be able to get more than two words out of the president. "You lose" were the only words he spoke to her.

Richard Nixon's (1969–74) mother, who named her son after King Richard the Lionheart, originally wanted him to be a Quaker missionary.

> **Franklin Pierce** (1853–57) was the first president to have a Christmas tree in the White House.

When Franklin D. Roosevelt (1933–45) was five years old, he visited the White House and was told by the then president, Grover Cleveland (1885–89), "My little man, I am making a strange wish for you: it is that you may never be president of the United States." It is also worth noting that Roosevelt's mother dressed him exclusively in girl's clothing until the age of five.

Another example of a president's meeting a future president came in 1963, when Bill Clinton (1993–2001) shook hands with John F. Kennedy (1961–63) at a White House reception for members of Boys' Nation.

William Henry Harrison (1841) was the first president to die in office.

Martin Van Buren (1837–41) was the first president to be born a U.S. citizen.

Gerald Ford (1974–77) was the only president never to have been elected as either president or vice president.

Grover Cleveland (1885–89; 1893–97) was the only president elected to two nonconsecutive terms.

John Quincy Adams (1825–29) used to take a swim in the Potomac River every morning—naked.

Zachary Taylor (1849–50) moved around the country so much that he never managed to register to vote. Consequently, the first time he voted, he was sixty-two years old.

John Tyler (1841–50) was the first president to marry in office.

James A. Garfield (1881) was the only man in U.S. history to be simultaneously a congressman, a senator-elect and a president-elect.

Gerald Ford (1974–77) and Bill Clinton (1993–2001) were both adopted as children.

George Washington was the only president not to belong to a political party. He was also the only president to be elected unanimously. In the 1820 election, James Monroe (1817–25) would have won every electoral vote, but a New Hampshire delegate didn't want Washington to lose this distinction and so didn't vote for Monroe.

James Madison (1809–17) was the first president to wear long trousers. All the previous presidents had worn knee breeches.

Famous People Who Were Adopted

Bill Clinton, Ray Liotta, Eric Clapton, Gerald Ford, Kiri Te Kanawa, Debbie Harry, Axl Rose, James Michener, Bo Diddley, Art Buchwald, Edward Albee, Art Linkletter, Wesley Clark, Frances McDormand

Famous Women Who Adopted Children

Nicole Kidman, Julie Andrews, Jamie Lee Curtis, Frances McDormand, Sharon Stone, Calista Flockhart, Drew Barrymore, Diane Keaton, Michelle Pfeiffer, Mia Farrow, Kiri Te Kanawa, Kirstie Alley, Patricia Kluge, Pearl Bailey, Connie Francis, Jane Russell, Barbara Stanwyck, Valerie Harper, Gloria Swanson, Lisa Lopes

Famous Women Who Put Their Babies Up for Adoption

Roseanne, Joni Mitchell, Linda Lovelace

Famous Only Children

Shannon Elizabeth, Marilyn Manson, Craig David, Adrien Brody, Teri Hatcher, Elton John, Bob Hoskins, Uri Geller, Robert De Niro, Clive James, Harold Pinter, Charlotte Church, Jean-Paul Gaultier, Jacques Chirac, Sarah Michelle Gellar, Barbara Taylor Bradford, David Copperfield, Martina Hingis, Sam Mendes, Burt Bacharach, Anthony Hopkins, Peter Ustinov, Lauren Bacall

People Who Died on Their Birthday

Raphael (April 6, 1483/1520—and for good measure both days fell on Good Friday)

William Shakespeare (April 23, 1564/1616, though there is some doubt over his precise date of birth)

Ingrid Bergman (August 29, 1915/1982)

Kings and Their Unfortunate Nicknames

King Rudolf the Sluggard (Rudolf III, king of Burgundy from 993 to 1032)

King Malcolm the Maiden (Malcolm IV, king of Scotland from 1153 to 1165)

King Louis the Fat (Louis VI, king of France from 1108 to 1137)

King Ferdinand the Fickle (Ferdinand I, king of Portugal from 1367 to 1383)

King Charles the Mad (Charles VI, king of France from 1380 to 1422)

King Ivan the Terrible (Ivan IV, king of Russia from 1547 to 1584)

King Louis the Stubborn (Louis X, king of France from 1314 to 1316)

King Charles the Bad (Charles II, king of Navarre from 1349 to 1387)

King Henry the Impotent (Henry IV, king of Castile from 1454 to 1474)

King Ethelred the Unready (Ethelred II, king of England from 978 to 1016)

Kings and Their Fortunate Nicknames

King Louis the Just (Louis XIII, king of France from 1610 to 1643)

King William the Good (William II, king of Sicily from 1166 to 1189)

King Philip the Handsome (Philip, king of Castile in 1506; he was married to Joan the Mad)

King Charles the Victorious (Charles VII, king of France from 1422 to 1461)

King Henry the Saint (Henry II, king of Germany from 1014 to 1024)

King Richard the Lionheart (Richard I, king of England from 1189 to 1199)

King Philip the Fair (Philip IV, king of France from 1285 to 1314)

King Ferdinand the Great (Ferdinand I, king of Castile from 1035 to 1065)

King Charles the Wise (Charles V, king of France from 1364 to 1380)

King Louis the Well-Beloved (Louis XV, king of France from 1715 to 1774)

Famous People and the Age at Which They Lost Their Virginity

Casanova (11)

Harold Robbins (11)

Jimi Hendrix (12)

Don Johnson (12)

Johnny Depp (13)

James Caan (13)

George Michael (13—heterosexual sex)

Gillian Anderson (13—"I feel very ashamed looking back on it. It was only when I reached about 22 that I realized you could actually enjoy sex.")

Mae West (13)

Bob Geldof (13)

Jon Bon Jovi (13)

Anton Chekhov (13)

Clint Eastwood (14—with a "friendly neighbor")

David Duchovny (14)

James Joyce (14)

Cher (14)

Phil Collins (14—in a garden plot)

Bruce Willis (14—"I was a 14-year-old bellboy at a Holiday Inn, and it was the most incredible experience of my life. This really gorgeous chick started coming on to me, so we went down to the laundry room together. She guided me through it, and things got kind of hot down there.")

Kate Moss (14)

Natalie Wood (14)

King Charles II (15—with his former wet nurse)

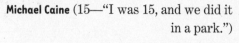

Michael Caine (15—"I was 15, and we did it in a park.")

Stephen Fry (15—with a girl named Shelagh while listening to "American Pie")

Charlie Sheen (15—with a prostitute. "The problem was she wanted four hundred dollars, so we used my dad's credit card.")

Dustin Hoffman (15—with a girl who thought he was his older brother. "She was a nymphomaniac called Barbara. She was 19 and I was 15½. My brother Ronnie threw a New Year's Eve party. It was over before it began, but she thought she was making love to my brother, and when she realized it was me, she screamed and ran out naked.")

Björk (15)

Madonna (15—in the back of a Cadillac with a guy named Russell)

Jerry Hall (15—to a rodeo rider who kept his boots on)

Brigitte Bardot (16—with Roger Vadim)

John F. Kennedy (17)

Lee Evans (17—with the woman who became his wife)

Geri Halliwell (17—to a boy called Toby, "a sickly looking ex-public-school boy with a toffy accent")

Joan Collins (17—"I was 17, and he was 33. It was just like my mother said—the pits.")

Victoria Beckham (17)

Walt Disney (18—on his birthday)

Barbra Streisand (18)

Brad Pitt (18)

Jamie Lee Curtis (18)

Napoleon Bonaparte (18)

Brooke Shields (18—with Dean Cain)

Cliff Richard (18—with Carol Harris, the wife of Jet Harris of the Shadows)

Jeffrey Archer (18—in the woods)

Leonardo DiCaprio (18)

Marlon Brando (19—with an older Colombian woman)

Mira Sorvino (20)

Victor Hugo (20)

Queen Victoria (21)

Dudley Moore (22)

Edvard Munch (22)

H. G. Wells (22)

D. H. Lawrence (23)

Elliott Gould (23—with Barbra Streisand)

Mariah Carey (23)

John Cleese (24)

Isadora Duncan (25)

Bette Davis (26)

Alfred Hitchcock (27)

William Gladstone (29)

George Bernard Shaw (29)

Lisa Kudrow (31—"I'm glad I waited till I was married. I decided my virginity was precious, an honor I was bestowing on a man.")

Mark Twain (34)

People with Roses Named After Them

Paul McCartney, Prince Philip, Tina Turner, Jane Asher, Julie Andrews, Michael Crawford, Cliff Richard

Real People Mentioned in Beatles Songs

Queen Elizabeth II ("Penny Lane" and "Mean Mr. Mustard")

Edgar Allan Poe ("I am the Walrus")

Harold Wilson and Edward Heath ("Taxman")

B. B. King, Doris Day and Matt Busby ("Dig It")

Charles Hawtrey ("Two of Us")

Mao Tse-tung ("Revolution")

Sir Walter Raleigh ("I'm So Tired")

Peter Brown ("The Ballad of John and Yoko")

Bob Dylan ("Yer Blues")

The Infinite Wisdom of Mark Twain

"There are several good protections against temptation, but the surest is cowardice."

"Always do right. This will gratify some people and astonish the rest."

"**When angry,** count to four; when very angry, swear."

 "**A flea can be** taught everything a congressman can."

"**It takes your enemy** and your friend—working together—to hurt you to the heart: the one to slander you and the other to get the news to you."

"**I can live** for two months on a good compliment."

"**I was born modest.** Not all over, but in spots."

"**I am opposed to** millionaires—but it would be dangerous to offer me the position."

"**Fewer things are harder** to put up with than the annoyance of a good example."

"**Man is the** only animal that blushes—or needs to."

"**If you tell the truth,** you don't have to remember anything."

"**I must have a** prodigious quantity of mind; it takes me as much as a week, sometimes, to make it up."

"**Man: a creature made** at the end of the week's work when God was tired."

"**Such is the human race,** often it seems a pity that Noah didn't miss the boat."

"**Education is what** you must acquire without any interference from your schooling."

"**Familiarity breeds** contempt . . . and children."

"**The public is** the only critic whose opinion is worth anything at all."

"Confession may be good for my soul, but it sure plays hell with my reputation."

"Good breeding exists in concealing how much we think of ourselves and how little we think of the other person."

"Wit is the sudden marriage of ideas which, before their union, were not perceived to have any relation."

"Life would be infinitely happier if we could only be born at the age of eighty and gradually approach eighteen."

"Noise proves nothing. Often a hen who has merely laid an egg cackles as if she had laid an asteroid."

"Courage is resistance to fear, mastery of fear, not absence of fear."

"It is better to deserve honors and not have them than to have them and not deserve them."

"We may not pay Satan reverence, for that would be indiscreet, but we can at least respect his talents."

"What a good thing Adam had— when he said a good thing, he knew nobody had said it before."

The Adventures of Barry Humphries

Before finding fame as Dame Edna Everage, Humphries was a Dadaist who performed a series of stunts in the name of art.

On his frequent flights between Australia and Britain, Humphries would pass the time by surreptitiously putting some Russian salad (chopped and diced vegetables in mayonnaise) in a sick bag and then, when other passengers were watching, he would pretend to throw up into the bag. He would then proceed to eat its contents. Humphries didn't restrict this "gag" to airplanes but also performed it to a wider public. He would put some Russian salad on the pavement and then return to it later and eat it with a spoon. Once, in London in the 1960s, a policeman approached him but was so sickened that he started retching. Humphries took the opportunity to disappear.

One of his favorite tricks was to get a female co-conspirator to dress up as a schoolgirl. The two of them would start kissing, and when a policeman showed up to ask him what he was doing with a "minor," he would flourish her birth certificate proving that she was, in fact, over eighteen.

One particularly unpleasant stunt was performed—like many of his others—on a train. His friend would board a train pretending to be blind, with his leg in a cast and wearing a neck brace. Humphries would then get on board pretending to be a German and start abusing his friend, physically and verbally. Humphries was never challenged by other passengers. Meanwhile, after he got off, his friend would sit there saying, "Forgive him, forgive him."

For another stunt, Humphries would fill a public trash can with rubbish, and then, just before it reached the top, he would put in some really expensive food— smoked salmon, cooked chicken, champagne—and cover this with a layer of rubbish. When people arrived, Humphries, dressed as a tramp, would astonish them by rummaging in the bin and pulling out fabulous delicacies.

In 1968, when movies were infested with a plague of ludicrous avant-garde films, Humphries invented a "film director" named Martin Agrippa, who had supposedly been working with the Blind Man's Cinema and who had made a film that had won the "Bronze Scrotum" in Helsinki. Together with the (genuine) film director Bruce Beresford, he made a spoof film that was subsequently exhibited at several festivals of underground cinema, where it was taken entirely seriously.

With a group of friends, Humphries used to go to a shop every day at the same time and pay for a bar of Lux soap but never take the soap away. They would sometimes get strangers to do the same thing. Each time the shopkeeper would say, "You've forgotten your soap," to which Humphries and company would respond, "We don't want the soap, we just want to buy it!" Eventually Humphries took the soap out of the shop but returned, saying, "I'm sorry, I forgot to leave the soap." The shopkeeper eventually moved to another part of town.

One of Humphries's greatest stunts was performed while he was a university student. He took his seat on a Melbourne commuter train. At the first stop, one of his pals boarded the train and served him a grapefruit. At the next stop, another pal took away the grapefruit and gave him cornflakes. And so on—through the eggs and bacon and the coffee—until he had been served a full breakfast.

Famous People with Famous Ancestors

Mike Myers—William Wordsworth

Patricia Cornwell—Harriet Beecher Stowe

Gena Lee Nolin—Isaac Newton

Kyle MacLachlan—Johann Sebastian Bach

Cate Blanchett—Louis Blériot

Tom Hanks—Abraham Lincoln

Glenn Ford—President Martin Van Buren

Prince Philip—Queen Victoria

Helena Bonham Carter—Herbert Asquith

Judy Garland—President General Ulysses S. Grant

Barbara Cartland—Robert the Bruce

William Holden—President Warren G. Harding

General Colin Powell—King Edward I

Basil Rathbone—King Henry IV

Richard Nixon—King Edward III

Holly Valance—Benny Hill (Benny was Holly's grandfather's cousin)

Christopher Plummer—former Canadian prime minister Sir John Abbott (he's the great-grandson)

Famous People Born on the Very Same Day As Other Famous People

George Foreman and Linda Lovelace—1/10/49

Eartha Kitt and Roger Vadim—1/26/28

Charles Darwin and Abraham Lincoln—2/12/1809

Jerry Springer and Stockard Channing—2/13/44

Alan Bates and Barry Humphries—2/17/34

Robert Mugabe and Sam Peckinpah—2/21/25

Mikhail Gorbachev and Tom Wolfe—3/2/31

Prince Edward and Neneh Cherry—3/10/64

Michael Caine and Quincy Jones—3/14/33

Lara Flynn Boyle and Sharon Corr—3/24/70

John Major and Eric Idle—3/29/43

Marlon Brando and Doris Day—4/3/24

Francis Coppola and David Frost—4/7/39

Andre Agassi and Uma Thurman—4/29/70

Albert Finney and Glenda Jackson—5/9/36

Bono and Merlene Ottey—5/10/60

Jonathan Pryce and Ronnie Wood—6/1/47

famous people born on the very same day as other famous people

Stacy Keach and Charlie Watts—6/2/41

Matthew Broderick and Rosie O'Donnell—3/21/62

Meryl Streep and Lindsay Wagner—6/22/49

John Cusack and Mary Stuart Masterson—6/28/66

Diana, Princess of Wales, and Carl Lewis—7/1/61

Sylvester Stallone and President George W. Bush—7/6/46

Diana Rigg and Natalie Wood—7/20/38

Angela Bassett, Belinda Carlisle and Madonna—8/16/58

Christian Slater and Edward Norton—8/18/69

Chrissie Hynde and Julie Kavner—
9/7/51

Goran Ivanisevic and Stella
McCartney—9/13/71

Tommy Lee Jones and Oliver Stone—9/15/46

Ernie Els and Wyclef Jean—10/17/69

Dannii Minogue and Snoop Dogg—10/20/71

Hillary Rodham Clinton and Jaclyn Smith—
10/26/47

Rebecca Romijn-Stamos and Thandie Newton—
11/6/72

Daryl Hannah and Julianne Moore—12/3/60

John Denver and Ben Kingsley—12/31/43

Collectors Of . . .

Old photographs (Brian May)

Dolls' houses and furniture (Judi Dench)

1940s typewriters (Tom Hanks)

Porcelain pigs (Janet Jackson)

Shirley Temple memorabilia (Melissa Joan Hart)

Antique toys (Dustin Hoffman)

Literary autographs (Tom Stoppard)

Art—particularly Victorian nudes (Ozzy Osbourne)

Beanie Babies (Nick Carter)

Vintage Polaroid cameras (Brendan Fraser)

Dried insects—which she paints and frames (Claudia Schiffer)

Antique watches (Nicolas Cage)

Toilet seats (Prince Charles)

Chairs (Brad Pitt)

Puppets (David Arquette)

Medical prosthetics, such as eyes and limbs; vintage metal lunch boxes (Marilyn Manson)

Inflatable ducks (Kim Basinger)

Coat hangers (Penelope Cruz)

Snakes (Slash)

Thimbles (José Carreras)

Perfume bottles (Helena Christensen)

Old board games based on TV shows (Quentin Tarantino)

People Who Launched Their Own Fragrances

Linda Evans—*Forever Krystle*

Dame Elizabeth Taylor—*White Diamonds, White Diamonds Brilliant, White Diamonds Sparkling, Black Pearls, Diamonds & Emeralds, Diamonds & Rubies, Diamonds & Sapphires, Forever Elizabeth, Passion*

Engelbert Humperdinck—*Release Me*

Omar Sharif—*Omar Sharif*

Sophia Loren—*Sophia*

Björn Borg—*Signature*

Cynthia Lennon—*Cynthia Lennon's Woman*

Joan Collins—*Scoundrel*

Luciano Pavarotti—*Luciano Pavarotti Parfum for Men*

Catherine Deneuve—*Deneuve*

Naomi Campbell—*Naomi*

Jennifer Lopez—*J. Lo Glow, Still*

Christina Aguilera—*Fetish*

Isabella Rossellini—*Manifesto*

Céline Dion—*Eau de Céline Dion*

Stella McCartney—*Stella*

Paloma Picasso—*Paloma Picasso*

Sarah Jessica Parker—*Lovely*

Britney Spears—*Fantasy*

People Who Launched Their Own Products

Burt Reynolds—jewelry

Joan Collins—jeans

Paul Newman—salad dressing, tomato sauces, etc.

Jerry Hall—swimwear

Princess Stephanie of Monaco—swimwear

Ken Kercheval—popcorn

Joan Rivers—jewelry

Iman—cosmetics

Bo Derek—shampoos, conditioners and fragrances for dogs (the brand name is Bless the Beast)

Kelly LeBrock—Kelly LeBrock's Homeopathic Remedy Kit for Kids

Jaclyn Smith—perfume and clothing

Clint Eastwood—Pale Rider Ale

Elle Macpherson—designer lingerie

Ted Nugent—beef jerky

Jay-Z—clothing

Marie Osmond—cosmetics, porcelain dolls and clothing patterns

Christina Aguilera—cosmetics

Sadie Frost—clothing

Jennifer Lopez—clothing ($10 million deal with Tommy Hilfiger's younger brother)

Carlos Santana—shoes that "radiate rhythm, passion and energy"

Chaka Khan—chocolates

Kylie Minogue—lingerie

Missy Elliott—lipstick called Misdemeanor Lipstick

Busta Rhymes—clothing

Jane Seymour—clothing

People Who Insured Parts of Their Body

Michael Flatley—legs for $40 million

Bruce Springsteen—voice for $5 million

Dolly Parton—bust for $3 million

Jamie Lee Curtis—legs for $1 million

Keith Richards—third finger of left hand for £1 million

Jennifer Lopez—body for $1 billion

Tina Turner—lips for $1 million and breasts for $750,000

Mariah Carey—body for $1 billion

Guest Editors of French *Vogue*

The Dalai Lama, Alfred Hitchcock, Nelson Mandela, Federico Fellini, Joan Miró, Princess Caroline of Monaco, Salvador Dalí, Orson Welles, David Hockney, Martin Scorsese, Marc Chagall, Mikhail Baryshnikov, Roman Polanski

Guest Editors of Other Magazines

Cherie Blair—*Prima*

Mario Testino—*Visionaire*

Joan Collins—*Marie Claire* (UK)

Isabelle Huppert—*Cahiers du Cinéma*

Gwyneth Paltrow—*Marie Claire* (United States)

Jennifer Saunders and Joanna Lumley—*Marie Claire* (UK)

Susan Sarandon—*Marie Claire* (United States)

Roseanne—*New Yorker, National Enquirer*

Geri Halliwell—*New Woman*

Jerry Springer—*Chat*

Leonardo DiCaprio—*National Geographic* children's magazine

Famous People with Famous Aunts

Jemma Redgrave—Vanessa Redgrave

Macaulay Culkin—Bonnie Bedelia

Alessandra Mussolini—Sophia Loren

Bridget Fonda—Jane Fonda

George Clooney—Rosemary Clooney

Famous People with Famous Uncles

Ewan McGregor—Denis Lawson

Nicolas Cage—Francis Coppola

Parents of Twins

Donald Sutherland, Phil Silvers, George W. Bush, Denzel Washington, Al Pacino, Robert De Niro, Ivan Lendl, Jane Seymour, James Galway, Gary Oldman, Pele, Pat Cash, Alan Bates, Margaret Thatcher, Mel Gibson, Mark Knopfler, Cybill Shepherd, James Stewart, Ingrid Bergman, Bing Crosby, Mia Farrow, Günter Grass, Madeleine Albright, Corbin Bernsen, Lou Diamond Phillips, Ed Asner, Henry Mancini, Rick Nelson, Meredith Baxter, Jim Brown, Andy Gibb (himself the brother of twins), Susan Hayward, Loretta Lynn, Otto Preminger, Nelson Rockefeller

People with a Twin Brother/Sister

Scarlett Johansson (Hunter)

Gisele Bundchen (Patricia)

Alanis Morissette (Wade)

Joseph Fiennes (Jake)

Vin Diesel (Paul)

Isabella Rossellini (Ingrid)

Pier Angeli (Marisa)

Tim Gullikson (Tom)

Kiefer Sutherland (Rachel)

Jerry Hall (Terry—sister)

Men Who Had Twins Who Died at Birth or in Childhood

Elvis Presley, Liberace, William Randolph Hearst, Ed Sullivan, Edgar Allan Poe, Leonardo da Vinci, Lewis Carroll, Oscar Wilde, Justin Timberlake (twin sister, Laura, died minutes after birth)

Andy Garcia was born with a partly formed twin on his shoulder.

People Who Came from Large Families

Tim Allen (one of 10 children)

Rosie Perez (one of 10 children)

Mel Gibson (one of 11 children)

Benny Goodman (one of 11 children)

Lewis Carroll (one of 11 children)

Glen Campbell (one of 11 children)

Dolly Parton (one of 12 children)

Little Richard (one of 12 children)

George Burns (one of 13 children)

Perry Como (one of 13 children)

Little Eva (one of 13 children)

Richard Burton (one of 13 children)

Nicolae Ceausescu (one of 13 children)

Céline Dion (one of 14 children)

Charles Bronson (one of 15 children)

Billy Blanks (one of 15 children)

Sonny Liston (one of 25 children)

People Who Have/Had a Famous Father-in-Law

Woody Allen—André Previn

Jonny Lee Miller and Billy Bob Thornton—Jon Voight

Barry Humphries—Sir Stephen Spender

Anthony Quinn—Cecil B. DeMille

Axl Rose—Don Everly

Charlie Chaplin—Eugene O'Neill

Richard Wagner—Franz Liszt

Belinda Carlisle—James Mason

David Frost—the Duke of Norfolk

John McEnroe—Ryan O'Neal

Shannen Doherty—George Hamilton

Peter Lawford—Dan Rowan and Joseph Kennedy Sr.

Artie Shaw—Jerome Kern

Oskar Werner—Tyrone Power

Geraldo Rivera—Kurt Vonnegut Jr.

W. H. Auden—Thomas Mann

Burt Lancaster—Ernie Kovacs

David O. Selznick—Louis B. Mayer

Daniel Day-Lewis—Arthur Miller

P. J. O'Rourke—Sidney Lumet

Tony Blair—Anthony Booth

Lauren Holly—Anthony Quinn

Jeremy Irons—Cyril Cusack

George Clooney—Martin Balsam

Arnold Schwarzenegger—Sargent Shriver

Woody Harrelson—Neil Simon

People Who Have/Had A Famous Mother-in-Law

Liam Neeson—Vanessa Redgrave

Sidney Lumet—Lena Horne

Gary Oldman—Ingrid Bergman

Martin Scorsese—Ingrid Bergman

Cousins

Christopher Lee and Ian Fleming

Ginger Rogers and Rita Hayworth

Whitney Houston and Dionne Warwick

Natasha Richardson and Jemma Redgrave

Rip Torn and Sissy Spacek

Carole Lombard and Howard Hawks

Lauren Bacall and Shimon Peres

People Who Overcame a Stammer

Bruce Willis, Carly Simon, Winston Churchill, Harvey Keitel, King George VI, Sam Neill, James Earl Jones, W. Somerset Maugham, Marilyn Monroe, Charles Darwin, Arnold Bennett, Lewis Carroll

What Famous People Did in World War II

Dirk Bogarde served as a captain in the Queen's Royal Regiment and saw action in France, Germany and the Far East. He also helped to liberate the Nazi concentration camp of Belsen.

Denholm Elliott served in the RAF until being shot down in a bombing mission over Denmark. He was captured and sent to a POW camp in Silesia for the last three years of the war. He gave a hugely praised performance as Eliza Doolittle in the camp production of *Pygmalion*.

Kirk Douglas was a lieutenant in the U.S. Navy and saw action in the Pacific before internal injuries suffered in combat led to an early discharge.

Peter Ustinov served as a private in the Royal Sussex Regiment before being transferred to the position of David Niven's batman so that they could collaborate on the film *The Way Ahead*.

Richard Todd served with the Light Infantry, the Parachute Regiment and the Sixth Airborne Division seeing action on D Day and in the Battle of the Bulge.

Sammy Davis Jr. served in the U.S. Army but was bullied by white southerners—five of whom once painted him white. However, he was taught to read by a black sergeant.

Edmund Hillary served as a navigator in the Royal New Zealand Air Force in the Pacific.

Burt Lancaster served as a private in the American Fifth Army, having enlisted immediately after Pearl Harbor.

Ian Fleming served as assistant to the director of Naval Intelligence. After D Day he was put in charge of Assault Unit No. 30, which was known as Fleming's Private Navy.

Walter Matthau served in the U.S. Army in France (where he lost his virginity).

Tony Curtis served in the U.S. Navy in the Pacific, where he witnessed the Japanese surrender.

Donald Pleasence declared himself to be a conscientious objector at the start of the war and was sent to the Lake District to work as a forester. However, he had a change of heart and joined the RAF. He was shot down in France and spent the last year of the war in a German POW camp.

Alec Guinness served in the Royal Navy in Combined Operations and captained a ship.

Marilyn Monroe worked in a defense plant while her then husband (James Dougherty) went into the merchant marine.

Audrey Hepburn starved in occupied Holland, living on two loaves of bread for one month.

Rod Steiger lied about his age to join the U.S. Navy as a torpedoman on a destroyer in the South Pacific and saw action at Iwo Jima.

James Stewart saw active service as a pilot in the U.S. Air Force with the rank of colonel.

Dick Francis served as a pilot officer in the RAF, flying Lancaster and Wellington bombers.

Christopher Lee served in the RAF as a flight lieutenant and with Intelligence and Special Forces in the Western Desert, Malta, Sicily, Italy and Central Europe. He was mentioned in dispatches in 1944.

Tony Bennett served with the U.S. Army in Europe as an infantryman.

Eli Wallach served in the U.S. Army Medical Corps and helped battle casualties in Europe.

Peter Sellers was in the Entertainments Division of the RAF.

Leslie Nielsen joined the Royal Canadian Air Force and trained as an air gunner, but the war ended before he could see combat.

David Tomlinson served as a Flight Lieutenant in the RAF.

Larry Adler gave recitals for the Allied troops in Europe.

Aaron Spelling served in the U.S. Army Air Force and was awarded the Bronze Star and Purple Heart with Oak Leaf Cluster.

Ian Carmichael served as a major in the Twenty-second Dragoons in northwest Europe, gaining a mention in dispatches.

Telly Savalas served with the U.S. Army toward the end of the war and was injured in action.

Rossano Brazzi joined the Italian Resistance after his parents were murdered by the Fascists. He also continued to make films during the war.

Dinah Shore traveled more miles than any other American entertainer to entertain the troops.

Dr. Timothy Leary was expelled from West Point after a drinking incident that led to a court-martial. However, he went on to become an army psychologist.

Jeff Chandler served in the army in the Pacific, rising from infantryman to first lieutenant.

President George Bush was the U.S. Navy's youngest-ever fighter pilot. He flew fifty-eight missions and was once shot down (and rescued). He won five medals.

Prince Philip served in the Royal Navy and captained a ship.

Lorne Greene served in the Royal Canadian Air Force.

Martin Balsam served in the U.S. Army Combat Engineers before transferring to the U.S. Army Air Force.

Robert Altman was a bomber pilot in the Pacific.

Johnny Carson served with the U.S. Naval Reserve.

People Who Attended the Same Schools

Neil Diamond and Barbra Streisand (Erasmus Hall High School, New York)

Cameron Diaz and Snoop Dogg (Long Beach Polytechnic High School),

Ben Kingsley and Robert Powell (Manchester Grammar, Manchester)

Mick Fleetwood and Jeremy Irons (Sherborne, Dorset)

P. G. Wodehouse and Raymond Chandler (Dulwich, London)

Judi Dench and Margaret Drabble (The Mount, York)

Robert Redford and Stacy Keach (Van Nuys High School, California)

Indira Gandhi and Iris Murdoch (Badminton, Bristol)

Ann-Margret and Bruce Dern (New Trier High School, Illinois)

Tony Blair and Rowan Atkinson (Durham Choristers Preparatory School, Durham)

Hugh Grant and Alan Rickman (Latymer Upper, London)

People Who Were Bullied at School

Gwyneth Paltrow (because she was "gawky")

Harrison Ford (because he "liked to hang out with girls")

Gillian Anderson (because of her "independent" and "bossy" attitude)

Prince Charles (because he was heir to the throne—was especially bullied during rugby games)

Mel Gibson (because of his American accent at his Australian school)

Sandra Bullock (because she was "ugly")

Tom Cruise (because he "was always the new kid in town")

Michelle Pfeiffer (because of her "big lips")

Sophie Dahl (by a boy who fancied her but whom she rejected)

Whitney Houston (because her "hair was too straight" and her "skin was too white")

Woody Allen (because of his name, Allen Konigsberg—"I'd tell them my name was Frank, but they'd still beat me up")

Kate Winslet ("I was mentally bullied"—because of her weight)

Patrick Swayze (because he liked to dance)

Ralph Fiennes ("for being a poof")

Jude Law (at a state school in southeast London; he moved to a private school, where he was also bullied)

Christina Aguilera (because she appeared on TV). In 2000, she got back at one of the bullies by driving in her sports car to the McDonald's where the girl worked. "I heard you were working here and wanted to say hello," she said.

Eminem (because his mom used to move all the time)

Victoria Beckham (because of her wealthy background; girls at school would push her around and swear at her in the playground and call her names because she had acne)

Ricky Martin (became the victim of a school bully named Manuel at the age of ten. He used to push him around and goad him into fighting, but he never fought back.)

Robert Carlyle (because he had no shoes and long hair)

Winona Ryder (because of her androgynous look)

Natalie Imbruglia ("for having big lips and big eyes")

People Who Were Bullies (Self-Confessed) at School

Stella McCartney, David Schwimmer, Martin Amis

People Who Were Educated at Home

Agatha Christie, C. S. Lewis, Yehudi Menuhin, Alexander Graham Bell, Queen Elizabeth II, George Bernard Shaw, Britney Spears, Joaquin Phoenix, the Everly Brothers

People and Their Nicknames from School Days

Prince William—Wombat

George Michael—Yog

Kate Moss—Mosschops

Cindy Crawford—Crawdaddy

Kate Winslet—Blubber

Steven Spielberg—The Retard

Michael Caine—The Professor

Cameron Diaz—Skeletor (because she was so skinny)

Elle Macpherson—Smelly Elly

Rebecca Romijn-Stamos—Jolly Blond Giant

Victoria Beckham—Acne Face

Ricky Martin—Kiki (this is also slang in Asia for "pussy")

Geri Halliwell—Pancake (because of her flat chest)

Thom Yorke—Salamander (on account of his "weird, wonky, reptile eyes")

Leonardo DiCaprio—The Noodle

Rowan Atkinson—Moon Man, Doopie and Zoonie

Puff Daddy—Born Sean Combs, he was given the nickname Puff because, as a child, he would huff and puff when angry

Sophia Loren—The Stick or Toothpick (because she was so thin)

Will Smith—The Prince (given to him by a teacher because of his regal attitude)

Denise Richards—Fish Lips

Kate Hudson—Hammerhead Shark (her brother's nickname because of the space between her eyes)

Jeff Goldblum—Bubwires ("because I had braces on my teeth when nobody else did, and I think they were saying 'barbed wires'")

Justin Timberlake—Brillo Pad (because of his curly locks)

Robert De Niro—Bobby Milk (because he was so white)

Nicole Kidman—Stalky

Kylie Minogue—Shorty

Gisele Bundchen—Oli (short for Olive Oyl, because she was so tall and skinny)

Britney Spears—Boo-Boo

Elijah Wood—Little Monkey

Natalie Imbruglia—Jagger Lips and Frog Eyes

Benjamin Bratt—Scarecrow (because he was so thin)

People Who Were Expelled from School

Nicolas Cage (from elementary school, for putting dead grasshoppers in the egg salad on picnic day)

Guy Ritchie (from Stanbridge Earls School near Andover, for being in a girls' room or for snorting sulphate on Sports Day—depending on whether you listen to his father or to him)

Macy Gray (from boarding school, after, she says, reporting a dean who made improper physical contact)

Dan Aykroyd (from St. Pius X Preparatory Seminary, for committing acts of "minor" delinquency)

Salma Hayek (from a Louisiana boarding school, for setting alarm clocks back three hours)

Marilyn Manson (from a private conservative Christian school)

Kevin Spacey (from a military academy, for hitting a classmate with a tire)

Gabriel Byrne (from a seminary, after being caught smoking in a graveyard)

Martin Amis (from Battersea Grammar, for blowing off school at the age of fourteen for a few months to play a part in the film *A High Wind in Jamaica*)

Roger Daltrey (from Acton Grammar School, for smoking and refusing to wear the school uniform)

Boy George (from Eltham Green School, for—according to his headmaster—"not coming to school and not working")

Jackie Collins (from Francis Holland School, for smoking)

Stephen Fry (from Uppingham, for theft)

Matthew Modine (from at least two high schools)

Jim Broadbent (from Leighton Park, just before his A-level exams, for drinking)

People Who Dropped Out of College

Michael Douglas, Richard Dreyfuss, Carly Simon, Bill Cosby, Warren Beatty, Mick Jagger, Jane Fonda, Candice Bergen, Matt Damon, Christie Brinkley, Kate Beckinsale, Bill Gates

People and Their Classmates' Ratings

Billy Crystal—voted Wittiest Student

Tom Cruise—voted Least Likely to Succeed

Sylvester Stallone—voted Most Likely to End Up in the Electric Chair

Sandra Bullock—voted Most Likely to Brighten Your Day

Robin Williams—voted Least Likely to Succeed

Meg Ryan—voted Cutest Girl in Class

Gillian Anderson—voted Girl Most Likely to Go Bald (because of her hairstyles) and Most Likely to Be Arrested

Halle Berry—voted Prom Queen, but was forced to share the title with a "white, blond, blue-eyed, all-American girl"

Matthew Fox—voted Most Likely to Appear on *Hee Haw*

Eddie Murphy—voted Most Popular

Chris Tucker—voted Most Humorous

John Leguizamo—voted Most Talkative

People Who Went to Finishing School

Minnie Driver

Anne Robinson

Zsa Zsa Gabor

Film Gaffes

In *Charlie's Angels* **(2000),** when Drew Barrymore lifts up Lucy Liu to spin her around and kick the baddie, Drew calls out "Lucy!" to get her attention—even though Lucy Liu's character's name is Alex. See also *The Doors* (1991), when Meg Ryan calls Val Kilmer "Val" instead of "Jim," his character's name, and *The War of the Roses* (1989), in which Michael Douglas addresses Danny DeVito's character as "DeVito."

In *Rear Window* **(1954),** James Stewart has a cast on his leg for the whole film, which is fine, except that in one scene the cast switches legs.

In *The Bible* **(1966),** the actor playing Adam has a belly button. . . .

In *Spider-Man* **(2002),** Peter shoots his web at a lamp and pulls it across the room, smashing it, but seconds later it's back on the dresser in one piece.

In *Robin Hood: Prince of Thieves* **(1991),** the sheriff uses the expression "ten-thirty." Clocks didn't exist in the twelfth century.

In *Commando* **(1985),** the Porsche is wrecked on the left side—until Arnie drives it away and it's fine.

In *Harry Potter and the Sorcerer's Stone* **(2001),** at the start-of-term feast, Harry sits down on one side of the table next to Ron. When the food is served, Harry is on the other side of the table, next to Hermione.

In *Austin Powers in Goldmember* **(2002),** we learn that Austin Powers left school in 1959. This means that the family holiday in Belgium, when he was a baby, would have been between 1941 and 1944 when Belgium was occupied by the Nazis.

In *The Bridge on the River Kwai* **(1957),** Alec Guinness—who won an Oscar for his role—has his name spelled with just one *n* in the final credits. Christopher Walken also had his name misspelled: in the credits of *Annie Hall* (1977).

In *The Perfect Storm* **(2000),** when the men are watching movies, there's a copy of *Blade Runner (Director's Cut)* on the table. The director's cut was released in 1992, but this movie is set in 1991.

In *Gladiator* **(2000),** in a battle scene, a chariot is turned over and a gas cylinder can be seen in the back.

In *The Maltese Falcon* **(1941),** as Sam Spade (Humphrey Bogart) slaps Joel Cairo (Peter Lorre), the latter's bow tie changes from polka dots to stripes.

In *Speed* **(1994),** Harry (Jeff Daniels) is shot by Jack (Keanu Reeves) in the left leg, but we later see him limping on the right leg.

In *The Wedding Singer* **(1998),** Julia's wedding was supposed to take place on Sunday, August 5, 1985. But in 1985, August 5 fell on a Monday.

In *The Last Temptation of Christ* **(1988),** you can see the label in Christ's robe.

In *It's a Wonderful Life* **(1946),** the old man's cigar disappears when he sends young George to deliver a prescription.

In *Spartacus* **(1960),** you can clearly see a vaccination scar on the arm of Spartacus (Kirk Douglas).

In *The Silence of the Lambs* **(1991),** Clarice Starling (played by Jodie Foster) has blue eyes, but the actress playing her as a child has brown eyes.

In *My Best Friend's Wedding* **(1997),** when Jules is trying on her dress, she's wearing a white bra with a visible strap. Later this becomes a black bra.

In *Pearl Harbor* **(2001),** Kate Beckinsale is seen wearing a bikini—even though the bikini wasn't invented until 1946 (five years later).

In *The Commitments* **(1991),** Imelda (Angeline Ball) decides not to go off with her family on a camper holiday to the Isle of Man. Unfortunately for her family (who does go), the Isle of Man bans campers.

In *48 Hours* **(1982),** Eddie Murphy is handcuffed when he leaves jail. The handcuffs then disappear but later reappear.

O Brother, Where Art Thou? **(2000)** shows George "Babyface" Nelson on his way to the electric chair. But George Nelson was never arrested in Mississippi, and anyway he wasn't executed but was killed by police near Chicago.

In *Born on the Fourth of July* **(1989)** you can hear "American Pie," but this was released three years after the film was set.

In *The Matrix Reloaded* **(2003),** there is a scene during a power outage where car headlights also go out.

Opera

Key dates in the history of opera: 1597—the first opera (Peri's *Dafne*); 1637—the first public opera house opened in Venice; 1778—La Scala was built; 1865—Wagner wrote *Tristan und Isolde*.

The longest operas—including intervals—performed at the Royal Opera House are all written by Wagner and are *Götterdämmerung* (6 hours), *Die Meistersinger von Nurnberg* (5 hours, 40 minutes), *Siegfried* (5 hours, 25 minutes).

The shortest opera ever performed is *The Deliverance of Theseus* (Darius Milhaud—7 minutes, 27 seconds).

Famous opera haters include Jean Jacques Rousseau, George Bernard Shaw and Voltaire.

Things said about opera: "Opera is when a guy gets stabbed in the back and, instead of bleeding, he sings" (Ed Gardner); "Going to the opera, like getting drunk, is a sin that carries its own punishment with it and that a very severe one" (Hannah More); "Opera is like a husband with a foreign title: expensive to support, hard to understand, and therefore a supreme social challenge" (Cleveland Amory); "People are wrong when they say the opera isn't what it used to be. It is what it used to be. That's what's wrong with it" (Noël Coward).

Most curtain calls received by an opera singer: 165 (Luciano Pavarotti in 1988 in Berlin).

Extraordinary Middle Names

Joan **Henrietta** Collins

Rowan **Sebastian** Atkinson

Mel **Columcille** Gibson

Gene **Alden** Hackman

Woody **Tracy** Harrelson

Rob **Hepler** Lowe

Joseph **Alberic** Fiennes

Geri **Estolle** Halliwell

Quincy **Delight** Jones

Kate **Garry** Hudson

Leonardo **Wilhelm** DiCaprio

Russell **Ira** Crowe

John **Marwood** Cleese

Uma **Karuna** Thurman

Hugh **John Mungo** Grant

Ben **Geza** Affleck

Robbie **Maximilian** Williams

Richard **Tiffany** Gere

Noah **Strausser Speer** Wyle

Courteney **Bass** Cox

Famous Women Whose Real First Name Is Mary

Lauren Hutton, Barbara Cartland, Dusty Springfield, Kathleen Turner, Debbie Reynolds, Lily Tomlin, Dorothy Lamour, Sissy Spacek, Bo Derek, Meryl Streep, Debra Winger, Farrah Fawcett, Tipper Gore, Mae West

Famous People Who Use Their Middle Name As Their First Name

David Jude Law

Laura Reese Witherspoon

Keith Rupert Murdoch

Marvin Neil Simon

Ruz Fidel Castro

Mary Debra Winger

Olive Marie Osmond

Walter Bruce Willis

Charles Robert Redford

Roberta Joan (i.e., Joni) Mitchell

William Bradley Pitt

George Ivan (i.e., Van) Morrison

Henry Warren Beatty

Michael Sylvester Stallone

Dorothy Faye Dunaway

Christina Brooke Shields

Thomas Sean Connery

Rosalie Anderson (i.e., Andie) MacDowell

People Named After Someone/Something Famous

Halle Berry (after the Halle Brothers department store)

Christopher Walken (named Ronald—a first name he dropped—after the actor Ronald Colman)

Heath Ledger (after Heathcliff in *Wuthering Heights*)

John Leguizamo (after the actor John Saxon)

Natasha Richardson (after the heroine in Tolstoy's *War and Peace*)

Charisma Carpenter (after an Avon perfume)

Dido (after the African warrior queen)

Marilyn Monroe—born Norma Jean Baker (after the actress Norma Talmadge)

Dustin Hoffman (after the cowboy star of the silent movies Dustin Farnum)

Mariel Hemingway (after a bay in Cuba)

Sugar Ray Leonard (after the musician Ray Charles)

Whitney Houston (after the American TV soap star Whitney Blake)

Shirley Maclaine and Shirley Jones (after Shirley Temple)

Chelsea Clinton (after the song "Chelsea Morning")

Martina Hingis (after the tennis star Martina Navratilova)

Bette Midler (after the actress Bette Davis)

Oprah Winfrey (after Orpah, from the Bible's Book of Ruth; it was misspelled on her birth certificate)

Penelope Cruz (after the song "Penélope" by Joan Manuel Serrat)

Sadie Frost (after the song "Sexy Sadie" by the Beatles)

Céline Dion (after the song "Céline" by Hugues Aufray)

Unusual Names Famous People Have Given Their Children

Homer—Matt Groening

Kidatia—Quincy Jones

Bria—Eddie Murphy

Happy—Macy Gray

Jaden Gil—Steffi Graf and Andre Agassi

Denim—Toni Braxton

Jermajesty (boy)—Jermaine Jackson

Moon Unit, Dweezil, Diva and Emuukha Rodan—Frank Zappa

Dandelion (now Angela)—Keith Richards

Rain—Richard Pryor

Elijah Blue and Chastity Sun—Cher

Dakota Mayi—Don Johnson and Melanie Griffith

Navarone—Priscilla Presley

Dog—Sky Saxon

Rumer Glenn, Scout Larue and Tallulah Belle—Bruce Willis and Demi Moore

Brooklyn (girl)—Donna Summer

Brooklyn and Romeo (boys)—Victoria and David Beckham

Satchel—Spike Lee

Satchel—Woody Allen

Piper Maru—Gillian Anderson

Starlite Melody—Marisa Berenson

Memphis Eve and Elijah Bob Patricius Guggi Q—Bono

Zowie (now Joey)—David Bowie

Sailor Lee—Christie Brinkley

Phoenix Chi—Mel B

Free—Barbara Hershey and David Carradine

Kansas—David Carradine

Tyson—Neneh Cherry

Braison Chance and Destiny Hope—Billy Ray Cyrus

Morgana—Morgan Freeman

Skylar—Sheena Easton

Arrana and Blue Angel—The Edge

Colton Jack—Chris Evert

Atiana Cecilia—Oscar de la Hoya

Chiara-Charlotte—Catherine Deneuve and Marcello Mastroianni

Lily-Rose Melody—Johnny Depp and Vanessa Paradis

Mallory Loving—Rick Derringer

Gracie Fan—Danny DeVito and Rhea Perlman

Caleb—Jack Nicholson

Brawley King—Nick Nolte

Gulliver—Gary Oldman

Morgane—Roman Polanski

Maesa—Bill Pullman

Elettra-Ingrid—Isabella Rossellini

Justice—Steven Seagal

Sage Moonblood—Sylvester Stallone

Amadeo—John Turturro

Ocean and Sonnet—Forest Whitaker

Mercedes—Val Kilmer and Joanne Whalley

Chance Armstrong—Larry King

Samaria—LL Cool J

Rainie—Andie MacDowell

Arpad Flynn and Aurelius Cy—Elle Macpherson

Speck Wildhorse—John Cougar Mellencamp

unusual names famous people have given their children

William True—Kirstie Alley

Camera—Arthur Ashe

Erika, Erinn, Ensa, Evin and Ennis—Bill Cosby

Lolita and Piper—Brian De Palma

Chudney—Diana Ross

Gib and Prima—Connie Sellecca

Jesse Mojo—Sam Shepard

China—Grace Slick

Paris and Brielle—Blair Underwood

Rio—Sean Young

Victoria Kafka—Tommy Lee Jones

Cuathemoc—Louis Malle

Shelby—Reba McEntire

Imani—Jasmine Guy

Kenya—Quincy Jones and Nastassja Kinski

Atherton—Don Johnson

Paris—Michael Jackson

Paris—Pierce Brosnan

Eja—Shania Twain

And also: George Foreman named all five of his sons George. And he also has a daughter named Georgetta.

People Who Changed Their Names

Elton John (Reginald Dwight)

Meg Ryan (Margaret Hyra)

Alice Cooper (Vincent Furnier)

Ricky Martin (Enrique Morales)

Joan Rivers (Joan Molinsky)

Woody Allen (Allen Konigsberg)

Martin Sheen (Ramon Estevez)

Macy Gray (Natalie McIntyre)

Hammer (Stanley Burrell)

Engelbert Humperdinck (Gerry Dorsey)

Bono (Paul Hewson)

Bo Derek (Mary Cathleen Collins)

Calvin Klein (Richard Klein)

David Copperfield (David Kotkin)

Bill Wyman (William Perks)

Omar Sharif (Michael Shalhoub)

James Garner (James Baumgarner)

David Bowie (David Jones)

Jodie Foster (Alicia Foster)

Pat Benatar (Patricia Andrejewski)

Barry Manilow (Barry Pincus)

Michael Keaton (Michael Douglas)

Theresa Russell (Theresa Paup)

Carmen Electra (Tara Leigh Patrick—advised by Prince to change: Carmen after the opera and Electra after the goddess)

Eminem (Marshall Mathers III)

Queen Latifah (Dana Owens)

Tom Cruise (Thomas Cruise Mapother IV)

Ice Cube (O'Shea Jackson)

Donna Karan (Donna Faske)

Larry King (Lawrence Zeiger)

Nathan Lane (Joseph Lane)

Ralph Lauren (Ralph Lifshitz)

Spike Lee (Shelton Lee)

Courtney Love (Courtney Menely)

Toni Morrison (Chloe Wofford)

Ozzy Osbourne (John Michael Osbourne)

Bernadette Peters (Bernadette Lazzara)

Tim Allen (Tim Allen Dick)

Snoop Dogg (Cordozar Broadus)

Shania Twain (Eilleen Twain)

Wynonna Judd (Christina Ciminella)

Puff Daddy (Sean Combs)

Marilyn Manson (Brian Warner—he named himself after Marilyn Monroe and Charles Manson)

Jay-Z (Shawn Carter)

Joaquin Phoenix (Joaquin Bottom—his surname was changed by his parents, which suggests that his older brother, the late actor River Phoenix, was once named River Bottom)

Shaggy (Orville Burrell)

Stockard Channing (Susan Williams Antonia Stockard)

Eric Clapton (Eric Clapp)

Tina Turner (Annie Mae Bullock)

Doris Day (Doris Kapelhoff)

Axl Rose (William Bailey)

Michael Barrymore (Michael Parker)

Whoopi Goldberg (Caryn Johnson)

Billy Idol (William Broad)

Meatloaf (Marvin Aday)

Chevy Chase (Cornelius Chase)

Grandmaster Flash (Joseph Saddler)

Elle Macpherson (Eleanor Gow)

Tom Jones (Thomas Woodward)

Demi Moore (Demetria Guynes)

Winona Ryder (Winona Horowitz)

Jane Seymour (Joyce Frankenberg)

Christian Slater (Christian Hawkins)

Michael Caine (Maurice Micklewhite)

Sigourney Weaver (Susan Weaver—took the name from her favorite book, *The Great Gatsby*)

Elvis Costello (Declan McManus)

Julie Andrews (Julia Wells)

Anne Bancroft (Anna Italiano)

Mel Brooks (Melvin Kaminsky)

Charles Aznavour (Shahnour Aznourian)

Iggy Pop (James Osterburg)

Stevie Wonder (Steveland Judkins)

Diane Keaton (Diane Hall)

Jennifer Jason Leigh (Jennifer Morrow)

The Edge (David Evans)

Nicolas Cage (Nicholas Coppola)

Jack Palance (Walter Palanuik)

Tammy Wynette (Virginia Pugh)

Sting (Gordon Sumner)

Janis Ian (Janis Fink)

Lou Reed (Louis Firbank)

Tony Curtis (Bernard Schwartz)

Charles Bronson (Charles Buchinski)

Donna Summer (Donna Gaines)

Hulk Hogan (Terry Bollea)

Pink (Alecia Moore)

Aliases

Mr. Bellacon and Paul Cruise—Tom Cruise

Mr. Dripnoodle—Johnny Depp

Tipsy McStagger and Phil S. Stein—Robbie Williams

Mr. Hugh Jarse—George Michael

Miss Trixie Firecracker and Lili Paris—Geri Halliwell

Miss Flo Cha—Mel C

Claris Norman—Madonna

Pussy Jones—Dannii Minogue

Peter Gunn—Eminem

Bobby Dee—Kevin Spacey

A. N. Other—Prince Edward (in an Austrian hotel)

Sir Humphrey Handbag—Elton John

Miss R. Dynastar—Vanessa-Mae

Miss Cupcake—Mariah Carey

Sabrina Duncan—Shirley Manson

Miss Honey—Nicole Kidman

Bambi Shots—Anastacia

Mary Black—Courtney Love

John Doe—Keanu Reeves

Tom Feral—Kevin Costner

Sardines

The word _sardine_ refers to any of several species of small food
fish of temperate waters that are also known as
pilchards—especially when adult. Sardines are shoaling
fish that live near the surface feeding on plankton. This
ends the encyclopedia definition.

Sardines are sensitive fish. They move away from their shoaling grounds and don't return for decades after naval battles.

Sardines can improve your memory—according to a study of children in 1987. People with memory disorders have low levels of acetylcholine, which certain foods—such as sardines—can mitigate.

Sardines were sold for years in cans with keys that would inevitably break as you tried to turn them, leaving razor-sharp edges. This led to cut fingers, a lot of swearing, and oil going everywhere. In the past few years, they have been sold flat in cans with a ring-pull (like a soft drink) or standing up in a can which is opened with a can opener (like a can of baked beans). In the dark days of the old-style sardine-can key, nearly half of the shoppers surveyed complained about sardine-can keys breaking off or cutting them.

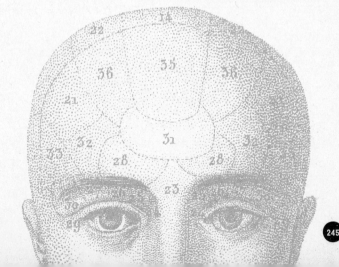

The Norwegian city of Stavanger uses as its symbol and crest the key to a tin of sardines.

In *Beyond the Fringe,* Alan Bennett described life as being "rather like a tin of sardines—we're all of us looking for the key."

Traditionally sardines were encouraged to rise to the surface of the sea by the fishermen drumming their feet on the bottom of the boat. The foaming shoals would then be scooped up in quantity.

In Britain, tinned sardines are one of the cheapest foodstuffs. If we want to describe someone as broke, they talk about them as living on a diet of sardines.

The French take sardines seriously. They sell prime-quality tinned sardines—skinned and boned, in extra-virgin olive oil—and even sell vintage sardines: date-stamped with the year they were captured, because good sardines improve in the can so long as the can is regularly turned. The French value sardines so highly that there was even a Pierre Cardin sardine can, and a museum totally dedicated to sardines, in Sete, features stuffed sardines, pictures of sardines and live sardines in tanks. The museum's creator said, "The fish are part of our culture."

According to a 1991 survey, 7 out of 10 men who eat a lot of canned fish—including sardines—head for the top and half rate themselves more successful than others. However, only 5 percent said they bounced back quickly after criticism, compared to 25 percent of non–fish eaters.

Like all oily fish, sardines (especially fresh ones) are marvelous for lowering cholesterol and are therefore an important guard against heart disease.

Sardines can help cancer sufferers. Trials at Edinburgh Royal Infirmary showed that a fatty acid in sardine oils prevents patients' losing weight by blocking a substance produced by tumors that destroys body tissue. This is important, because about half of cancer patients lose weight—some so severely that it kills them.

In Alexandria, Minnesota, no man is allowed to make love with the smell of sardines on his breath.

In Marseille, France, a 4,500-piece jigsaw puzzle depicting a two-acre sardine was laid out by thirty people in one week in 1992.

In 1995, millions of dead sardines were washed ashore along the Australian New South Wales coast when a mystery illness led to their suffocating after mucus blocked their gills.

In 1994, in Lima, Peru, 1,500 young people made a three-mile-long sardine sandwich in an attempt to get into the Peruvian *Guinness Book of Records*.

In Ipswich, Queensland, in Australia, sardines rained down from the sky in 1989. The fish were sucked up from the sea by a strong updraft of air and fell to the ground like hail. The local cats were said to be delighted.

There's the true story of the young boy who was told by his teacher to write about the harmful effects of oil on fish for his homework. He wrote, "My mummy opened a tin of sardines. The sardines were covered in oil and they were all dead."

The European Patents Office says that the most commonly requested item among its 31 million patent documents is sardine-flavored ice cream. A spokesman says, "No one believes that it actually exists until they've called it up and seen it themselves."

People Who Appeared in Commercials When They Were Children

Jodie Foster (Coppertone)

B. B. King (Pepticon health tonic)

Emma Bunton (Milky Bar)

Kate Winslet (Sugar Puffs)

Drew Barrymore (Gaines-burgers)

Mike Myers (Datsun)

Sarah Michelle Gellar (Burger King; she couldn't say "burger" and so needed a speech coach)

Patsy Kensit (Birds Eye frozen peas)

Melissa Joan Hart (Splashy—a bath toy)

Kirsten Dunst (a doll with bodily functions)

Yasmine Bleeth (was a Johnson & Johnson baby)

Jeff Daniels (McDonald's)

Rick Schroder (had appeared in about sixty ads by the age of seven)

Brooke Shields (was the Ivory Snow baby at the age of eleven months)

Christian Bale (Pac-Man cereal)

Jessica Biel (Pringles potato chips)

Reese Witherspoon (appeared in a TV commercial for a Nashville florist when she was seven)

Former Roommates

Tommy Lee Jones and Al Gore

Michael Caine and Terence Stamp

Lauren Holly and Robin Givens

M. Emmet Walsh and William Devane

Ewan McGregor and Jude Law

Joel and Ethan Coen, Frances McDormand and Holly Hunter

Marilyn Monroe and Shelley Winters

Charles Bronson and Jack Klugman

Charles Manson and Dennis Wilson

Cary Grant and Randolph Scott

Dustin Hoffman, Gene Hackman and Robert Duvall

David Niven and Errol Flynn

James Stewart and Henry Fonda

Michael Douglas and Danny DeVito

Mel Gibson and Geoffrey Rush

Matt Damon and
Ben Affleck

Nastassja Kinski and
Demi Moore

People and the Sports They Played

Shannon Elizabeth could have become a professional tennis player.

Matthew Perry was ranked number two at tennis in Ottawa at the age of thirteen.

Yanni was a member of the Greek national swimming team.

Kurt Russell left acting in 1971 to pursue a career in minor league baseball.

Hilary Swank swam in the Junior Olympics; she was also a top gymnast.

Queen Latifah was a power forward on two state championship basketball teams in high school.

Josh Hartnett turned to acting only after his soccer career ended.

George Clooney once tried out for the Cincinnati Reds baseball team.

Heath Ledger nearly became a professional ice-hockey player but chose acting over sports when given an ultimatum.

Gisele Bundchen originally wanted to be a professional volleyball player.

Allison Janney wanted to be a competitive figure skater, but a freak accident ended her chances.

Dr. Benjamin Spock won a rowing gold medal at the 1924 Olympics.

Tommy Lee Jones is a champion polo player.

Chevy Chase used to work as a tennis professional at a club.

Paul Newman once achieved second place in the grueling Le Mans 24 Hours Race.

Richard Harris won a Munster Cup medal playing in the second row for Garryowen in 1952 and might well have gone on to play Rugby Union for Ireland had he not contracted TB.

Richard Gere won a gymnastics scholarship to the University of Massachusetts.

Keanu Reeves was the goalie in his high-school ice-hockey team, where he earned the nickname "The Wall" and where he was voted MVP (most valuable player).

Arnold Schwarzenegger was not only a bodybuilding champion but also won the Austrian Junior Olympic Weightlifting Championship.

Julio Iglesias used to play goal for Real Madrid's second team.

Robert De Niro learned to box for his Oscar-winning role as Jake La Motta in *Raging Bull* and was so good that La Motta himself said that he could have taken it up professionally.

Bill Cosby was good enough at football to be offered a trial with the Green Bay Packers.

William Baldwin was a good enough player to have originally considered a professional baseball career with the New York Yankees.

Kirk Douglas once supplemented his meager earnings with professional appearances in the ring as a wrestler.

Billy Crystal attended college on a full baseball scholarship but decided not to pursue a career in the sport.

Peter O'Toole "distinguished himself on the rugby field" when he served in the navy in 1950–52.

Jim Brown embarked on an acting career only after having been a football star.

Davy Jones was an apprentice jockey before joining the Monkees; however, it was only after he retired from singing and made a racing comeback that he had his first win as a jockey.

Warren Beatty was offered scholarships as a football player by several universities but turned them all down to concentrate on acting.

Tom Cruise was an all-around sports star at school, but it was his wrestling that led to his acting career: he was on the school wrestling team but after injuring his knee turned to acting instead.

Jack Palance worked as a professional boxer—which was how he got the broken nose that helped him to earn parts playing the heavy.

Mickey Rourke had twenty-six amateur fights in the 1970s and then quit when his acting career took off; in recent years he has returned to the ring with some success.

Liam Neeson boxed for a local team from the age of nine until the age of seventeen (in one early match, his nose was broken and he had it set on the spot by his manager).

Sheryl Crow was a competitive hurdler.

Mel C ran for Cheshire county when she was a schoolgirl.

Alanis Morissette takes part in triathlons.

Sarah Michelle Gellar was a competitive figure skater for three years and was ranked third in New York State.

Geena Davis tried in 1999 to qualify for the U.S. Women's Olympic Archery team.

Ellen DeGeneres considered becoming a professional golfer.

Former Beauty Queens

Joan Blondell (Miss Dallas, 1926)

Dorothy Lamour (Miss New Orleans, 1931)

Zsa Zsa Gabor (Miss Hungary, 1936—stripped of the title for being too young)

Veronica Lake (Miss Florida, 1937—stripped of the title for being too young: "Being disqualified after you've won something is a pretty good way to lose.")

Lauren Bacall (Miss Greenwich Village, 1942)

Cloris Leachman (Miss Chicago, 1946)

Gina Lollobrigida (Miss Italy, 1946)

Marilyn Monroe (Miss California Artichoke Queen, 1947)

Vera Miles (Miss Kansas, 1948)

Debbie Reynolds (Miss Burbank, 1948)

Anita Ekberg (Miss Sweden, 1950)

Sophia Loren (Miss Elegance, 1950)

Shirley Jones (Miss Pittsburgh, 1952)

Imelda Marcos (Miss Manila, 1953)

Kim Novak (Miss Deepfreeze, 1953)

Raquel Welch (Miss Photogenic, 1953)

Dyan Cannon (Miss West Seattle, 1957)

Cybill Shepherd (Miss Teenage Memphis, 1966)

Shakira Caine (Miss Guyana, 1967)

Victoria Principal (Miss Miami, 1969)

Kim Basinger (Miss Junior Athens, 1969)

Oprah Winfrey (Miss Black Tennessee, 1971)

Lynda Carter (Miss World U.S.A., 1973)

Michelle Pfeiffer (Miss Orange County, 1976)

Sharon Stone (Miss Crawford County, 1976)

Marla Maples (Miss Resaca Beach Poster Girl, 1983)

Halle Berry (Miss U.S.A., 1986—first runner-up)

Helena Christensen (Miss Denmark, 1986)

Jeri Ryan (Miss Illinois, 1989)

Ali Landry (Miss U.S.A., 1996)

People Who Play/Played in Bands

Russell Crowe is in a band named 30 Odd Foot of Grunts.

Kevin Bacon formed the Bacon Brothers with his older brother, Michael.

Joe Pesci was lead vocalist with Joey Dee and the Starlighters.

Johnny Depp was in a series of garage bands, one of which (the Kids) opened for Iggy Pop; later he became a member of the band P (with Steve Jones of the Sex Pistols and Flea of the Red Hot Chili Peppers).

Gary Sinise formed the Bonsoir Boys in 1997.

Stephen King, Matt Groening, Dave Barry and Amy Tan are in a band called Rock Bottom Remainders.

David Lynch plays bass in a heavy metal group called Blue Bob.

Ricky Gervais sang in a band named Seona Dancing.

Richard Gere was the lead singer with the Strangers.

Kevin Costner was the vocalist with the group Roving Boy.

Diane Keaton sang with the Roadrunners.

Tony Blair was the lead singer in a university band, the Ugly Rumours.

Chevy Chase played drums for a college group that included Donald Fagen and Walter Becker of Steely Dan.

Patsy Kensit sang with Eighth Wonder.

Woody Harrelson is lead singer in the band Manly Moondog and the Three Kool Hats.

People Who Guested on Records

Peter Gabriel played flute on "Lady D'Arbanville" (Cat Stevens).

Rick Wakeman played synthesizer on "Space Oddity" (David Bowie).

Brian Jones played oboe on "Baby You're a Rich Man" (the Beatles).

Billy Joel played piano on "Leader of the Pack" (the Shangri-Las).

Elton John played piano on "He Ain't Heavy, He's My Brother" (the Hollies).

George Harrison played guitar on "Badge" (Cream).

Eric Clapton played guitar on "While My Guitar Gently Weeps" (the Beatles).

Paul Weller played guitar on "Champagne Supernova" (Oasis).

David Gilmour played guitar on "Wuthering Heights" (Kate Bush).

Stevie Wonder played harmonica on "I Feel for You" (Chaka Khan).

Johnny Depp played guitar on "Fade In-Out" (Oasis).

People and the Songs on Which They Sang Backup Vocals

David Bowie—"It's Only Rock and Roll" (the Rolling Stones)

Sheryl Crow—"Silver Girl" (Fleetwood Mac)

people and the songs on which they sang backup vocals

Eric Clapton—"All You Need Is Love" (the Beatles)

Rupert Everett—"American Pie" (Madonna)

George Michael—"Nikita" (Elton John)

Mick Jagger—"You're So Vain" (Carly Simon)

Phil Spector—"My Sweet Lord" (George Harrison)

Bruce Springsteen—"Street Hassle" (Lou Reed)

Luther Vandross—"Young Americans" (David Bowie)

Paul McCartney—"Mellow Yellow" (Donovan)

John Lennon—"Fame" (David Bowie)

Eric Clapton—"I Wish It Would Rain Down" (Phil Collins)

Sting—"Money for Nothing" (Dire Straits)

Michael Douglas—"When the Going Gets Tough (the Tough Get Going)" (Billy Ocean)

Billy Idol—"Dancin' Clown" (Joni Mitchell)

David Beckham—"Out of Your Mind" (Victoria Beckham—he sang on the first take which, apparently, wasn't subsequently used)

Roger Daltrey—"Bad Attitude" (Meat Loaf)

George Michael—"The Last Kiss" (David Cassidy)

Belinda Carlisle—"Pearl's Café" (the Specials)

Sting—"Shape" (Sugababes)

What They Did Before Becoming Famous

Geena Davis—live mannequin in a New York department store

Harvey Keitel—shoe salesman and court stenographer, having joined the U.S. Marines at the age of sixteen and served in Lebanon

Renée Zellweger—bartender's assistant

Lucy Lawless—worked in a gold mine

Huey Lewis—slaughtered rabbits: he had to hit them over the head with a pipe, then skin them and gut them

Beck—painted signs, moved refrigerators, took ID photos at the YMCA in New York, worked in a video store

Neve Campbell—ballerina

Hugh Grant—advertising account executive

Tom Clancy—insurance agent

George Clooney—sold insurance door to door, cut tobacco in Kentucky

Ellen DeGeneres—vacuum-cleaner saleswoman

Dennis Franz—postman ("the worst postman in the history of the Post Office")

Whoopi Goldberg—bricklayer, bank teller, makeup artist for a funeral parlor

John Goodman—bouncer

Dustin Hoffman—toy seller at Macy's, attendant in a psychiatric institution

Russell Crowe—bingo caller

Vin Diesel—bouncer

Matthew Modine—electrician, macrobiotic chef

Kevin Richardson—played a Ninja Turtle at the Disney–MGM Studios theme park

J. K. Rowling—worked at the Amnesty International office in London and then at the Chamber of Commerce in Manchester

Meg Ryan—journalist

Liam Neeson—forklift driver at the Guinness brewery in Belfast

Björk—fish-factory employee

Josh Hartnett—video-store clerk

Chris Isaak—funeral-parlor assistant

Nathan Lane—police bail interviewer

Peter Gabriel—milliner

Elvis Costello—computer programmer at the Elizabeth Arden factory

Tom Jones—glove cutter

Ben Kingsley—penicillin tester

Madonna—worked in Burger King; also as a lifeguard and an elevator operator

Robert Redford—pavement artist

Tina Turner—maid

Joe Cocker—plumber

Elton John—messenger boy

Willem Dafoe—magazine binder at *Penthouse*, also carpenter and electrician

Gloria Estefan—Spanish and French interpreter for customs at an American airport

Bill Withers—manufactured airplane toilet seats

Tom Hanks—bellhop

Kylie Minogue—video-shop worker

263

Jon Bon Jovi—Burger King worker

James Caan—rodeo rider

Kathy Bates—cashier in the gift shop in New York's Museum of Modern Art

Simon Le Bon—lumberjack

Mick Jagger—hospital porter

Cher—receptionist in a department store

Ozzy Osbourne—slaughterhouse laborer

Bob Hoskins—nightclub bouncer

Rod Stewart—gravedigger

Warren Beatty—cocktail-bar pianist

Jeremy Irons—social worker

Michelle Pfeiffer—supermarket assistant

Sean Connery—French polisher

Diana Rigg—coffee-bar assistant

Christie Brinkley—artist

Charlie Watts—designer in advertising

Paul Newman—encyclopedia salesman

Michael Caine—cement mixer, driller, meat porter

Rutger Hauer—electrician

Bob Newhart—accountant

Danny DeVito—janitor

Mickey Rourke—pretzel seller

Roger Daltrey—sheet-metal worker

Ringo Starr—bartender

Charlton Heston—artists' model

Diane Keaton—photographer

Drove Taxis

Pierce Brosnan, Michael Keaton, Alan Alda, Oliver Stone

Note also: Stephen Fry, Prince Philip, Andrew Lloyd Webber, Michael Jackson, John Wayne, Liberace and Woody Harrelson bought London cabs for their own personal use

Former Teachers

Sting, Bryan Ferry, Gabriel Byrne, Billy Crystal (substitute teacher), Luciano Pavarotti (elementary school), Oliver Stone (in Vietnam)

Worked as Lion-Cage Cleaners

Clive James, Sylvester Stallone

Worked as Waiters and Served Famous People

Richard Gere (once served Robert De Niro)

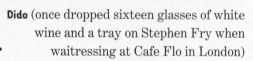

Dido (once dropped sixteen glasses of white wine and a tray on Stephen Fry when waitressing at Cafe Flo in London)

Served in the Israeli Army

Dr. Ruth Westheimer, Uri Geller, Debra Winger, Vidal Sassoon

Auditioned Unsuccessfully for the Monkees

Charles Manson, Stephen Stills

Former Hairdressers

Chuck Berry, Danny DeVito, Whoopi Goldberg

What They Originally Intended to Be

Whitney Houston—veterinarian

Mel Gibson—chef

Angelina Jolie—funeral director

Charisma Carpenter—teacher

Alec Baldwin—lawyer

Rowan Atkinson—electrical engineer

Eddie Izzard—accountant

Michael Palin—explorer

Jeremy Irons—veterinarian

Marilyn Monroe—schoolteacher

Agatha Christie—professional musician

Lynn Redgrave—cook

Dennis Quaid—musician

George Lucas—racing driver

Pope John Paul II—actor

William H. Macy—veterinarian

Julio Iglesias—lawyer

Tobey Maguire—chef

David Duchovny—a bathtub (he was six at the time)

Dustin Hoffman—concert pianist

Lisa Kudrow—doctor

Jennifer Lopez—hairstylist

J. C. Chasez—carpenter

Kathleen Quinlan—gymnastics teacher

Forest Whitaker—classical tenor

Lance Bass—astronaut (he passed the NASA exams)

Morgan Freeman—fighter pilot

Janet Jackson—lawyer

Emma Bunton—a pony (she was a young child at the time)

Ricky Gervais—a veterinarian (when he was seven)
and a marine biologist (when he was ten)

Ethan Hawke—news anchor

Claudia Schiffer—lawyer

Eminem—comic-book artist

Colin Farrell—soccer player

Julia Roberts—veterinarian

Alan Rickman—graphic artist

Miranda Richardson—veterinarian

Started Out as Secretaries

Sarah, Duchess of York

Belinda Carlisle

Shania Twain

Anne Robinson

Catherine Keener

Joan Allen

Trained as Ballet Dancers

Neve Campbell

Victoria Principal

Leslie Caron

269

Morgan Freeman

Charlize Theron

Jane Seymour (danced with the London Festival Ballet at the age of thirteen)

Mira Sorvino (performed in a professional production of *The Nutcracker* at the age of twelve)

Penélope Cruz

Sarah Jessica Parker (was with the Cincinnati Ballet and the American Ballet Theatre)

Trained to Be Doctors But Didn't Finish

Neil Diamond, Giorgio Armani, Lew Ayres (who went on to play Dr. Kildare), Robert Dole, Wim Wenders, Robin Givens, Dustin Hoffman, Bill Murray

People Who Lived in Their Cars

Brad Pitt

Lenny Kravitz (a Ford Pinto)

Hilary Swank (with her mother when she was a kid)

Bob Hoskins (in a Jeep after an expensive divorce)

Jim Carrey (at one point his family lived out of their car/trailer)

Genuine Car Bumper Stickers

CAUTION: I DRIVE JUST LIKE YOU!

DON'T DRINK AND DRIVE—YOU MIGHT SPILL SOME

THIS CAR IS INSURED BY THE MAFIA—YOU HIT ME, THEY HIT YOU

BE CAREFUL—90 PERCENT OF PEOPLE ARE CAUSED BY ACCIDENTS

SORRY, I DON'T DATE OUTSIDE MY SPECIES

REHAB IS FOR QUITTERS

NOT ALL DUMBS ARE BLOND

I TOOK AN IQ TEST, AND THE RESULTS WERE NEGATIVE

I DON'T BRAKE FOR PEDESTRIANS

IF YOU LIVED IN YOUR CAR, YOU'D BE HOME BY NOW

HONK IF YOU'VE BEEN MARRIED TO ELIZABETH TAYLOR

IF YOU THINK I'M A LOUSY DRIVER, YOU SHOULD SEE ME PUTT

LEARN FROM YOUR PARENTS' MISTAKES—USE BIRTH CONTROL

OF COURSE I'M DRUNK—WHAT DO YOU THINK I AM, A STUNT DRIVER?

EAT WELL, STAY FIT, DIE ANYWAY

YOU! OUT OF THE GENE POOL!

YOU CAN'T DRINK ALL DAY LONG IF YOU DON'T START FIRST THING IN THE MORNING

IF YOU DON'T LIKE THE WAY I DRIVE, GET OFF THE PAVEMENT

HOW MANY ROADS MUST A MAN TRAVEL DOWN BEFORE HE ADMITS HE IS LOST?

MY WIFE'S OTHER CAR IS A BROOM

I'M NOT A COMPLETE IDIOT—SOME PARTS ARE MISSING

HE WHO LAUGHS LAST THINKS SLOWEST

EX—SAUDI ARABIAN SHOPLIFTER—NO HAND SIGNALS

INSTANT ASSHOLE, JUST ADD ALCOHOL

BEER ISN'T JUST FOR BREAKFAST

Qualified Pilots

John Travolta, Greg Norman, Prince Charles, Kurt Russell, Kris Kristofferson, Gore Vidal (got his license at the age of ten), B. B. King, Treat Williams, Tom Cruise, John Grisham, Harrison Ford, Patrick Swayze

Toilets

Sir John Harington (1561–1612) invented the toilet for Queen Elizabeth I after she'd banned him from her court for circulating smutty stories. So she allowed him to return. Sir John's toilet did the job—up to a point—but there were unpleasant side effects.

The reason so many houses in England bear the legend "Queen Elizabeth I stayed here" is because she used to move on every time the stench became too much to bear.

273

The Victorian plumber, Thomas Crapper, perfected the system we all know and use: the siphon flush which, by drawing water uphill through a sealed cistern, is both effective and hygienic. Crapper was born in the village of Thorne: an anagram of throne. He also invented (and patented) the stair tread.

Toilet Facts

The most impossible item to flush is a Ping-Pong ball.

Psycho **was the first Hollywood film that** showed a toilet flushing—thereby generating many complaints.

The first toilet air freshener was a pomegranate stuffed with cloves.

The idea of separate cubicles for toilets is a relatively modern invention; the Romans, for example, sat down together in large groups.

In Victorian times, toilet seats were always made of wood: the well-to-do sat on mahogany or walnut, while the poor put up with untreated white pine.

The Victorians gave their johns names such as Cascade, Optimus, Alerto, Pluvius, Deluge, Tornado, Aquarius, Niagara, Planetas and the Subito.

The town council of Cheltenham Spa once voted to replace the words *Men* and *Women* on their public toilets with *Ladies* and *Gentlemen* in order to "attract a better class of person."

In the Middle Ages, "waste" from public latrines ran directly into the river or the sea.

When Queen Victoria visited Trinity College Cambridge, she looked down at the river Cam, which was basically an open sewer and, seeing the toilet paper, asked Dr. Whewell, the master of Trinity, what were all those pieces of paper floating down the river. The master replied, "Those, ma'am, are notices that bathing is forbidden."

Toilets Around the World

The Japanese have invented something called the Shower Toilet. Originally designed for invalids, it boasts a self-raising seat cover, a bidet, water jets, a heated seat, a hot-air dryer and a fan for the removal of smells, all operated with an infrared control. The Japanese have also built toilets that resemble coffee shops, churches and space stations, one that speaks your weight and one that is a bicycle.

In 1993, Juan Bernaus was sentenced to a three-year jail term in Argentina for switching the "Ladies" and "Gents" signs around on public toilets.

An American jeweler has built the world's most expensive toilet, made of gold, diamonds, rubies and emeralds, with a mink seat—it costs $175,000.

Toilet Paper

Before the invention of toilet paper, people used shells or stones, bunches of herbs or, at best, a bit of sponge attached to a stick, which they rinsed with cold water.

The Victorians were so delicate they couldn't bring themselves to use the words *toilet paper*; instead they said *curl papers*.

In 1986, Nathan Hicks of St. Louis, Missouri, shot his brother Herbert dead because he used six toilet rolls in two days.

The French use less toilet paper (8½ pounds per person per year) than any other European people; the Swedes use the most (18½ pounds, while the British are sixth in the European toilet-roll ranking with 10 pounds. In total the British use nearly 1.5 billion toilet rolls, more than 200,000 tons a year.

American civil servants' paychecks are recycled to make toilet rolls.

Hermann Göring refused to use regulation toilet paper and used to bulk-buy soft white handkerchiefs instead.

American researchers spent $100,000 on making the discovery that three out of four people hang their toilet rolls so that the paper is pulled down to be torn off rather than up.

The world's oldest piece of toilet paper—thought to be 1,200 years old—was found buried under an Israeli garage.

An American toilet manufacturer in California has created toilet rolls made from hay. It is not known whether this is the same Californian company that in 1992 started selling "camouflage" toilet paper for hunters to use so that fellow hunters don't mistake them for white-tailed deer.

Celebrities and Toilets

Judy Garland and Lenny Bruce both died on the loo; King George II died after falling off a loo.

In 1993, Barbra Streisand got stuck in a toilet at Liza Minnelli's apartment during a party; fellow guests **Jack Nicholson and Michael Douglas** couldn't break down the door, so the building's porter had to come up to release her.

Actor George Hamilton was once trapped in the toilet of a restaurant, but he was rescued after a few minutes.

Jack Nicholson has a dead rattlesnake embedded in the clear plastic seat of his toilet.

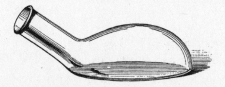

Winston Churchill did not believe in using toilet seats. He had them for his guests, but when his plumber asked him what sort of seat he would have on his own toilet, he responded, "I have no need of such things."

 In 1994, Chuck Berry installed video cameras in the women's toilets of his restaurant (The Southern Air).

Marti Pellow, the lead singer of Wet Wet Wet, was born in a public toilet in Clydebank.

People Who Have Been Pestered for Autographs in Toilets

Joan Collins stopped giving autographs after someone slid a piece of paper under a stall door and asked her to sign it.

Minnie Driver was also asked to give an autograph after someone slid a piece of paper under a stall, but merely said, "Could we do this outside?"

Andrea Corr was asked for an autograph while she was throwing up. "I couldn't believe it. I told her it might be a good idea if I washed my hands first."

Julia Roberts was asked for an autograph while she was on the john. She said, "I'm the tiniest bit busy."

Pierce Brosnan was asked while using a urinal. He obliged, but "I refused the guy's request to say 'shaken not stirred.'"

Toilet Quotes

"You must know that it is by the state of the lavatory that a family is judged." (Pope John XXIII)

"The biggest waste of water in the country by far. You spend half a pint and flush two gallons." (Prince Philip in a 1965 speech)

"Everything a man brings to his marriage is consigned to the downstairs loo." (Kelly Hoppen, an interior designer)

People and the Names They Gave Their Pets

Renée Zellweger: a dog (collie/retriever) named Dylan (which she nicknamed Woof or Woofer)

Britney Spears: two Yorkshire terriers named Mitzy and Baby, a Rottweiler named Cane and a poodle named Lady

Jessica Simpson: a pig named Brutus

Cameron Diaz: a cat named
The Little Man

Natalie Imbruglia: a dog (King
Charles spaniel) named Charlie

Ozzy Osbourne: dogs named
Baldrick (a bulldog), Sugar,
Sonny, Raider, Buster and
Phoebe

Samantha Mumba: a dog (shih tzu) named
Foxy

Sarah Michelle Gellar: a dog (Maltese terrier)
named Thor

Drew Barrymore: a dog named Flossie (once saved Drew's
life by waking her in a house fire)

Daniel Radcliffe: dogs (Border collies) named Binka
and Nugget

Courtney Love: a dog named Bob Dylan

Melissa Joan Hart: a duck named Flipper and dogs
named Holly Ochola and Permani
Pele

Axl Rose: a dog named Sumner
(Sting's surname at birth)

Julia Roberts: a dog named Gatsby

Matt LeBlanc: a dog (Doberman pinscher) named Shadow

Isabella Rossellini: a dog (dachshund) named Ferdinando

William Shatner: a dog (Doberman pinscher) named Kirk

Uma Thurman: a dog (chow chow) named Muffy

Steve Martin: a cat named Dr. Carlton B. Forbes

Victoria and David Beckham: dogs (Rottweilers) named Puffy and Snoopy

Jennifer Jason Leigh: dogs named Bessie and Otis

Kirsten Dunst: cats named Inky, Taz and Zorro

Hilary Swank: dogs named Lucky and Tanner, a rabbit named Luna, a parrot named Seuss and a cat named Deuce

Brendan Fraser: a dog (Chihuahua) named Lucy

Ralph Lauren: a dog (bearded collie) named Rugby

Valentino: dogs (pugs) named Molly and Maggie

Domenico Dolce and Stefano Gabbana: dogs (yellow Labradors) named Lola and Dalí

Giorgio Armani: cats—a Blue Russian named Uli and three Persians named Nerone, Micia and Charlie

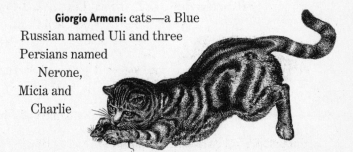

A. J. McLean: dogs (Yorkshire terriers) named Vegas and Jack Daniel's

Elizabeth Taylor: parrots named Dick and Liz

Leonardo DiCaprio: a dog (poodle) named Rufus

Jim Carrey: a dog (Labrador) named Hazel (who gets a professional massage three times a week and lives in a $20,000 three-room doghouse, complete with plush sofa)

George Michael: a dog (Labrador) named Hippy

Robbie Williams: a cat named Our Lady Kid

Madonna: a dog named Pepito

Geri Halliwell: a dog (shih tzu) named Harry

Adam Sandler: a dog (bulldog) named Meatball

Ringo Starr: dogs named Ying and Yang

Brad Pitt: a dog named Saudi

Brian Littrell: a dog (Chihuahua) named Little Tyke

Ali Landry: a dog (shih tzu) named Cosmo

Prince William: a dog named Widgeon

Charisma Carpenter: a dog (golden retriever) named Sydney

Mira Sorvino: a dog named Deer

Wolfgang Joop: dogs (Pomeranians) named Otto, Willy and Wolfie

Princess Stephanie of Monaco: a giraffe named Aisha

Reese Witherspoon: a dog (bulldog) named Frank Sinatra

Pamela Anderson: a dog (golden retriever) named Star

Liv Tyler: a dog named Neil

Mariah Carey: dogs (shih tzus) named Bing and Bong, (Jack Russell) named Jack, (Yorkshire terrier) named Ginger

Fears and Phobias

FLYING: Whitney Houston, Aaron Spelling, the Dalai Lama, Lenny Kravitz, Mike Oldfield, Bret Easton Ellis, Bob Newhart, Muhammad Ali, Joanne Woodward, Sam Shepard, Billy Bob Thornton, Whoopi Goldberg, Cher, Glenda Jackson, Aretha Franklin, Dina Carroll, Justin Timberlake, Joaquin Phoenix

GERMS AND/OR DIRT: Michael Jackson, Howard Hughes, Marlene Dietrich, Prince

CLOWNS: Billy Bob Thornton, Puff Daddy/P. Diddy, Johnny Depp

THE DARK: Christina Aguilera, Joan Collins, Margaret Thatcher, Stephen King

SNAKES: Sarah, Duchess of York; Madeleine Albright; Stephen King

EARTHQUAKES: Kevin Bacon, George Clooney

CATS: Julius Caesar, Napoleon, King Henry II

Other People and Their Fears and Phobias

Ernest Hemingway (telephones—because of his fear of the American income-tax office)

Madonna (thunder)

Rachel Weisz (frogs—she's been known to go without a bath rather than evict amphibian intruders from her ground-floor bathroom)

The Dalai Lama (caterpillars)

Billy Bob Thornton (antiques)

Kate Beckinsale (metaphobia—fear of throwing up)

Christina Ricci (gerbils)

Matthew McConaughey (tunnels and revolving doors)

Queen Christina of Sweden (fleas)

Sigmund Freud (train travel)

Queen Elizabeth I (roses)

Judy Garland (horses)

Alfred Hitchcock (policemen—he refused to learn to drive for fear of being stopped by a policeman)

Graham Greene (blood and bats)

Robert Mitchum (crowds)

Sid Caesar (haircuts)

Robert De Niro (dentists)

Natalie Wood (water—she was to die by drowning)

Lee Evans (the color green—he once freaked out when he was made to wear a green suit)

Famous People Who Bought Houses That Had Belonged to Other Famous People

Pete Townshend bought Ronnie Wood's house, The Wick, in Richmond, Surrey (which he'd bought from John Mills).

Engelbert Humperdinck bought Jayne Mansfield's house in Beverly Hills, California.

Burt Reynolds bought Al Capone's ranch in Florida.

Jacqueline Bisset bought Clark Gable and Carole Lombard's house in Benedict Canyon, California.

Noah Wyle bought Bo Derek's ranch in Santa Barbara, California.

Jerry Seinfeld bought Billy Joel's beachfront estate in the Hamptons.

John Cleese bought Bryan Ferry's Holland Park, London house.

Madonna bought Diane Keaton's Beverly Hills home.

Earl Spencer bought David Gilmour's West London house.

Gangsta rapper 50 Cent bought Mike Tyson's seventeen-acre estate in Farmington, Connecticut.

Brittany Murphy bought Britney Spears's Hollywood Hills house.

People and the Instruments They Can Play

PIANO: Dustin Hoffman, Anthony Hopkins, Clint Eastwood, Richard Gere, Rupert Everett, Warren Beatty, Chevy Chase

CLARINET: Woody Allen, Ricki Lake (also flute, piano and piccolo)

BANJO: George Segal, Ewan McGregor, Steve Martin

FRENCH HORN: Ewan McGregor, Samuel L. Jackson

GUITAR: Renée Zellweger, Serena Williams, Tony Blair, Minnie Driver, Gary Sinise (bass)

SAXOPHONE: Bill Clinton, James Gandolfini

TRUMPET: James Gandolfini, Samuel L. Jackson

CELLO: Prince Charles, Emily Watson

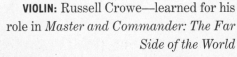

TUBA: John Malkovich

ACCORDION: Gabriel Byrne

MANDOLIN: Nicolas Cage—learned for his role in *Captain Corelli's Mandolin*

VIOLIN: Russell Crowe—learned for his role in *Master and Commander: The Far Side of the World*

HARMONICA: Dan Aykroyd

People Who Experienced Bad Stage Fright

Barbra Streisand returned to the stage after stage fright put her off. On her return she said, "It has taken me 2,700 hours and $360,000 worth of psychotherapy to be able to sing." Streisand puts her stage fright partly down to a PLO death threat in 1967, which caused her to forget her lines onstage.

Elvis Presley's hip wiggling started out as stage fright. According to Carl Perkins, "Elvis was so nervous his legs would shake. One day he did it, and the crowd went wild. He asked guitarist Scotty Moore, 'What'd I do?' and Moore replied, 'I don't know but do it again.' "

Derek Jacobi avoided the theater for two years after forgetting his lines as Hamlet in 1980.

Laurence Olivier went through a bout of terrible stage fright when he was running the National Theatre and playing Othello. Olivier said, "All I could see were the exit signs, and all I wanted to do was run off the stage each night towards them."

Barry Humphries suffers from stage fright "every night" and has to "overcome a tremendous reluctance to get on-stage."

Tim Roth started out as a stage actor on the fringe. Now he sticks to films because his stage fright leads him to having "nightmares" about the theater.

Marvin Gaye had such bad stage fright that he once tried to escape by climbing out of his dressing room.

Stephen Fry suffered such bad stage fright (as well as other problems) in *Cell Mates* that he left the country.

Uma Thurman has avoided stage work since 1996 after bursting into tears in an off-Broadway show.

Vanessa Redgrave was struck with panic while appearing in *The Prime of Miss Jean Brodie* and didn't perform onstage for another six years.

Téa Leoni had such bad stage fright while recording the pilot for *The Naked Truth* that she threw up five times.

In 2001, Robbie Williams announced he was going to take time off because he was suffering from stress and stage fright.

Judy Garland tried hypnosis but found that Irish whiskey worked better.

Minnie Driver has terrible stage fright and throws up into a bucket before public appearances.

William Hurt said, "Right before I go onstage, I sometimes vomit on myself and really make a mess."

Kristin Scott Thomas said, "People talk about butterflies—well, I had elephants."

Kissing

The first kiss was supposedly delivered by God. According to Genesis, God breathed the "spirit of life" into Adam. This has come to be interpreted symbolically as a kiss, which is why so many religious ceremonies include kissing.

A study by a Canadian anthropologist demonstrated that 97 percent of women shut their eyes during a kiss but only 37 percent of men did. The late actor Anthony Quinn had an explanation: "Many a husband kisses with his eyes wide open. He wants to make sure his wife is not around to catch him." Chico Marx (of the Marx Brothers) would have agreed. Chico was a habitual philanderer. When his wife caught him French-kissing a girlfriend, he replied, "I wasn't kissing her, I was whispering in her mouth."

Kissing on the lips is something the Romans started. A husband returning from work would kiss his wife's lips to see if she'd been drinking during the day. The Romans had three different types of kiss: *basium*, the kiss on the lips; *osculum*, a friendly kiss on the cheek, and *suavium*, the full monty. In fact, the Romans were so keen on kissing that Emperor Tiberius was obliged to ban the practice after an epidemic of lip sores. Until the Romans invaded, the British had no word for kissing.

The French kiss itself—tongues and all—was invented in the Brittany village of Pays de Mont as a substitute for sex because the population was growing too fast.

Kissing got bad press because of Judas Iscariot, who used the kiss as a sign of betrayal. In exchange for thirty pieces of silver, Judas identified Jesus to his enemies in the Garden of Gethsemane by kissing him. This is probably the earliest known example of kiss and tell.

In writing—particularly in greetings cards and in love letters—we use *XXXX*s to represent kisses. The origins of this go back to the days when people who couldn't write signed their name with an *X*. To emphasize their sincerity, they would then kiss their

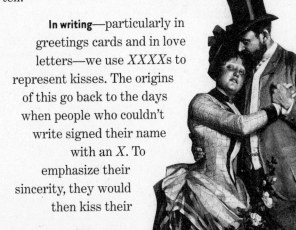

mark—in the same way that they would have kissed a Bible when swearing an oath on it. This practice of kissing the *X* led to the *X*'s representing a kiss. The Romans also sealed the signing of contracts with a kiss.

Kissing under the mistletoe at Christmas is an English tradition that has been exported to other countries. It started with the kissing bough, which had mistletoe at its center. When the Christmas tree replaced the kissing bough, the mistletoe was salvaged and given its own unique position in the Yuletide ritual.

Human beings are not the only mammals that kiss. Polar bears and kangaroos kiss. Chimpanzees can and do French-kiss. Sea lions rub mouths, a male mouse licks the mouth of a female mouse, and an elephant sometimes brushes its trunk against another elephant's lips.

Everyone knows that Lord Nelson said, "Kiss me, Hardy." However, some revisionists have claimed that what he really said was, "Kismet, Hardy," i.e., "fate." In fact, Hardy (an ancestor of Stan Laurel's partner, Oliver) understood him to say, "Kiss me," and that is what he duly did. Nelson said, "Now I am satisfied," and died about twenty minutes later, thanking God that he'd done his duty.

The Anti-Kissing League was formed in 1909 in America by people who considered kissing unhealthy.

How and where you kiss used to be a sign of where you stood in the social "pecking" order. Equals kissed each other on the cheek. The lower you ranked to another person, the lower you had to kiss him. Thus a slave would kiss his master's feet, and a prisoner—not allowed even that close—would be obliged to kiss the ground near the foot—i.e., kiss the dirt.

Rodin's *The Kiss* is one of the world's most important pieces of sculpture. The figure—completed in 1886—of two naked lovers kissing has not been entirely free from controversy. In the United States in the last century, it was deemed to be too explicit for the general public and was exhibited in a special room.

The most kissed statue in the world is not *The Kiss* but a marble statue of Guidarello Guidarelli, a sixteenth-century Italian soldier. At the end of nineteenth century, a rumor went around that any woman who kissed the statue would marry a fabulous man. Some 5 million kisses later, Guidarello's mouth is significantly redder than the rest of him.

One person who regretted kissing a work of art was Ruth van Herpen, who in 1977 was obliged to pay the restoration costs of a painting she had kissed and blighted with her red lipstick. In court she declared that she "only kissed it to cheer it up: it looked so cold."

Alice Johnson, a twenty-three-year-old American waitress, won a car in Santa Fe after kissing it for 32 hours and 20 minutes in a 1994 competition. She loosened four teeth in the process.

An American insurance company discovered that men were less likely to have a car accident on the way to work if they were kissed before they set off.

Mono is referred to as "the kissing disease" (because that is how it is easily spread among adolescents). In the United States, a person who has been fired is said to have been given the "kiss-off." A sailor who in olden times "kissed the gunner's daughter" had been tied to the breech of a cannon and flogged. A person vomiting is said to be "kissing the porcelain god."

As all Internet surfers know, the acronym KISS stands for "Keep It Simple, Stupid."

In Sicily, members of the Mafia have stopped kissing each other because the way they kissed was a dead giveaway to the police, and mobsters were getting arrested.

Screen Kisses

The first film kiss was in, appropriately enough, the 1896 movie *The Kiss*. The protagonists were John C. Rice and May Irwin.

The film with the most kisses is the 1926 *Don Juan*, in which John Barrymore performed 191 kisses with different women. This was before the 1930 Hays Code, which banned "excessive and lustful kissing."

Greta Garbo didn't relish kissing scenes with Fredric March, her costar in *Anna Karenina*, so she ate garlic before every such scene. Diana Rigg did the same before kissing George Lazenby in *On Her Majesty's Secret Service.* Julia Roberts hated kissing Nick Nolte while making *I Love Trouble*. At one point she sent a memo to the producer saying, "If he puts his tongue in my mouth one more time, I'm walking off the set."

Nepal bans films featuring kisses by Nepalese actors. The same is true of Bangladesh and Macao.

The most famous kiss in a Hollywood film is probably that between Burt Lancaster and Deborah Kerr in *From Here to Eternity*.

The first genuine French kiss in a Hollywood movie was between Warren Beatty and Natalie Wood in the 1961 film *Splendor in the Grass*.

The first kiss in an Indian film didn't take place until the 1978 film *Love Sublime,* when Shashi Kapoor and Zeenat Aman embraced. An Indian minister described the kissing scenes as "an insult" and called for a mass protest.

Bing Crosby—or so his costars claimed—had really bad breath, probably a result of his pipe smoking. Clark Gable's bad breath wasn't improved by the whiskey he regularly drank or the false teeth he wore, and Vivien Leigh hated having to kiss him in *Gone With the Wind.*

Kissing Around the World

Eskimos rub noses, as do a good many other peoples. Polynesians like a nose rub but also enjoy the *mitakuku,* which involves biting hairs from eyebrows. Trobriand islanders bite each other's eyelashes. In China they touch each other's cheeks and then sniff. In the Pacific Islands, they inhale each other's breath. In Gambia a man holds the back of a lover's hand against his nose.

After World War II, Americans were so keen to see the Japanese embrace the American way of life that during their occupation they ordered Japanese filmmakers to put kisses in their films. Some feat, in films that were invariably about Samurai warriors.

In Sorocaba, Brazil, they outlawed kissing in public places—specifically "the cinematographic kiss, in which salivas mix to swell the sensuality."

If you're in Scotland and are offered a "Glasgow kiss," or in Liverpool a "Kirby kiss," you'd better refuse unless you want a head butt.

Oliver Cromwell banned kissing on Sundays—even for married couples—on pain of a prison sentence.

In 1837, Thomas Saverland tried to kiss a woman who promptly bit off part of his nose. Saverland took her to court but lost, the judge commenting, "When a man kisses a woman against her will, she is fully entitled to bite his nose, if she so pleases."

In 1969, there was a mass kiss-in in the town of Inca on the island of Majorca. Young lovers were being fined 500 pesetas for kissing in public, so a group of couples held a "make-out-fest." The police charged them, and they were fined a total of 45,000 pesetas before being released.

Kissing and Health

The World Health Organization issued a warning against passionate kissing for World Aids Day, 1991—although current medical thinking is that you can't get AIDS from making out.

Kissing is good for your teeth. According to dentists, kissing encourages saliva, which acts as a mouthwash that helps prevent tooth decay. However, a 1994 report by the German Dental Association claimed that French kissing could give you a toothache on the grounds that "tongues can make holes in teeth."

Kissing can prevent illness. When you absorb other people's saliva, you also receive their enzymes, which gives you their immunities—a kind of antibiotic. Of course, kissing can pass on diseases, too.

Kissing a frog doesn't necessarily get you a prince, but it might get rid of your cold sore, thanks to a chemical secreted from frog skins.

A really tongue-twisting kissing session exercises 39 different facial muscles and can burn up 150 calories— more than a 15-minute swim. An ordinary peck uses up just 3 calories.

Things Said About Kissing

"Yet each man kills the thing he loves, . . . / The coward does it with a kiss, . . . / The brave man with a sword!" (Oscar Wilde, "The Ballad of Reading Gaol")

"What of soul was left, I wonder, when the kissing had to stop?" (Robert Browning)

"You must remember this, a kiss is just a kiss." (Dooley Wilson in *Casablanca*)

"I think less is more when it comes to kissing in the movies." (Julia Roberts)

"Sweet Helen, make me immortal with a kiss." (Christopher Marlowe, *Dr. Faustus*)

"People who throw kisses are hopelessly lazy." (Bob Hope)

"I kiss'd thee ere I kill'd thee: no way but this, / Killing myself, to die upon a kiss." (Shakespeare, *Othello*)

"Kissing don't last: cookery do!" (George Meredith)

"There is always one who kisses and one who only allows the kiss." (George Bernard Shaw)

UNICEF Ambassadors

Roger Moore, Julio Iglesias, Emmanuelle Béart, Edmund Hillary, Imran Khan, Liam Neeson, Richard Attenborough, Liv Ullmann, Peter Ustinov, Jane Seymour, Robbie Williams, Zinedine Zidane, Susan Sarandon, Nana Mouskouri, Michael Jackson, Jessica Lange, Laurence Fishburne, Harry Belafonte, Mia Farrow, Claudia Schiffer

Famous People and Their Allergies

Tom Cruise (cats)

Beyoncé Knowles (perfume)

Sandra Bullock (horses)

Clint Eastwood (horses)

Bill Clinton (flowers)

Richard E. Grant (alcohol)

Donald Sutherland (cigarette smoke)

Drew Barrymore (garlic and coffee)

Naomi Campbell (tuna)

Sharon Stone (caffeine)

Iggy Pop (milk)

David Cassidy (garlic)

Lleyton Hewitt (grass, horses and cats)

Kyle MacLachlan (wool)

Belinda Carlisle (wheat)

Rene Russo (sesame)

Celebrities and the Person They Chose as Their Best Man

Groom / Best Man

Uri Geller (renewing vows) / Michael Jackson

David Bailey / Mick Jagger

Kenneth Branagh / Brian Blessed

John McEnroe / Björn Borg

John Lennon / Brian Epstein

Bungee Jumpers

Leonardo DiCaprio, Zara Phillips, Pat Rafter, Andre Agassi, Debbie Harry, Renny Harlin, Prince William, Robbie Williams

Vineyard Owners

Cliff Richard, Peter Ustinov, Francis Coppola, Gerard Depardieu, Jean Tigana, Sam Neill, the Dalai Lama

Actors and the Roles They Turned Down

Vin Diesel turned down Ben Affleck's role in *Daredevil*.

Debra Winger turned down Glenn Close's role in *Fatal Attraction*.

Diane Lane turned down Renée Zellweger's role in *Chicago*.

John Travolta turned down Richard Gere's role in *Chicago*.

Kevin Costner turned down Matthew Broderick's role in *WarGames* (he did it to appear in *The Big Chill*, but his role in that was left on the cutting-room floor).

George Segal turned down Dudley Moore's role in *10*.

Robert Redford turned down Dustin Hoffman's role in *The Graduate*.

Lee Marvin turned down George C. Scott's role in *Patton*.

Sylvester Stallone turned down Eddie Murphy's role in *Beverly Hills Cop*.

George Raft turned down Humphrey Bogart's role in *The Maltese Falcon*.

Marlon Brando turned down Robert Redford's role in *Butch Cassidy and the Sundance Kid*.

Eddie Cantor turned down Al Jolson's role in *The Jazz Singer*.

Henry Fonda turned down Peter Finch's role in *Network*.

Elvis Presley turned down Kris Kristofferson's role in *A Star Is Born*.

Julia Roberts turned down Sharon Stone's role in *Basic Instinct*.

Robert De Niro turned down Willem Dafoe's role in *The Last Temptation of Christ*.

Richard Gere turned down Bruce Willis's role in *Die Hard*.

Harrison Ford turned down Michael Douglas's role in *Traffic*.

Susan Dey turned down Olivia Newton-John's role in *Grease*.

Al Pacino turned down Richard Gere's role in *Pretty Woman*.

Natalie Portman turned down Christina Ricci's role in *The Ice Storm*.

Kirsten Dunst turned down Mena Suvari's role in *American Beauty*.

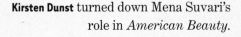

Cricket—as Explained to a Foreigner

You have two sides, one out in the field and one in.

Each man that's in the side that's in goes out, and when he's out, he comes in and the next man goes in until he's out.

When a man goes out to go in, the men who are out try to get him out, and when he is out, he goes in and the next man in goes out and goes in.

When they are all out, the side that's out comes in and the side that's been in goes out and tries to get those coming in, out.

Sometimes there are men still in and not out.

There are two men called umpires who stay out all the time, and they decide when the men who are in are out.

When both sides have been in and all the men are out (including those who are not out), then the game is finished.

All the Holders of the Miss World Title

2005: Unnur Birna Vilhjalmsdottir (Iceland)

2004: Maria Julia Mantilla Garcia (Peru)

2003: Rosanna Davison (Ireland)

2002: Azra Akin (Turkey)

2001: Agbani Darego (Nigeria)

2000: Priyanka Chopra (India)

1999: Yukta Mookhey (India)

1998: Linor Abargil (Israel)

1997: Diana Hayden (India)

1996: Irene Skliva (Greece)

1995: Jacqueline Aquilera (Venezuela)

1994: Aishwarya Rai (India)

1993: Lisa Hanna (Jamaica)

1992: Julia Kourotchkina (Russia)

1991: Ninibeth Jiminez (Venezuela)

1990: Gina Marie Tolleson (United States)

1989: Aneta Kreglicka (Poland)

1988: Linda Petursdottir (Iceland)

1987: Ulla Weigerstorfer (Austria)

1986: Giselle Laronde (Trinidad)

1985: Hofi Karlsdottir (Iceland)

1984: Astrid Herrera (Venezuela)

1983: Sarah-Jane Hutt (United Kingdom)

1982: Mariasela Lebrón (Dominican Republic)

1981: Pilin Leon (Venezuela)

1980: Kimberley Santos (Guam—after Gabriella Brum of Germany resigned)

1979: Gina Swainson (Bermuda)

1978: Silvana Suarez (Argentina)

1977: Mary Stavin (Sweden)

1976: Cindy Breakspeare (Jamaica)

1975: Winelia Merced (Puerto Rico)

1974: Anneline Kriel (South Africa—after Helen Morgan of the United Kingdom resigned)

1973: Marjorie Wallace (United States)

1972: Belinda Green (Australia)

1971: Lucia Petterle (Brazil)

1970: Jennifer Hosten (Grenada)

1969: Eva Reuber Staier (Austria)

1968: Penelope Plummer (Australia)

1967: Madeleine Hartog Bell (Peru)

1966: Reita Faria (India)

1965: Lesley Langley (United Kingdom)

1964: Ann Sidney (United Kingdom)

1963: Carole Crawford (Jamaica)

1962: Catharina Lodders (Holland)

1961: Rosemarie Frankland (United Kingdom)

1960: Norma Cappagli (Argentina)

1959: Corine Rottschafer (Holland)

1958: Penelope Coelen (South Africa)

1957: Marita Lindahl (Finland)

1956: Petra Schurmann (Germany)

1955: Carmen Zubillaga (Venezuela)

1954: Antigone Costanda (Egypt)

1953: Denise Perrier (France)

1952: May Louise Flodin (Sweden)

1951: Kiki Haakonson (Sweden)

Dishes from Around the World

Pig's Organs in Blood Sauce (Philippines)

Baked Bat (Samoa)

Crispy Roasted Termites (Swaziland)

Roast Field Mice (Mexico)

Weaver Moths in Their Nests (Zaire)

Parrot Pie (actually twelve budgerigars) (Australia)

Bee Grubs in Coconut Cream (Thailand)

Guinea Pig in a Creole Style (Peru)

Queen White Ants (South Africa)

Calf-Udder Croquettes (France)

Coconut-Cream-Marinated Dog (Indonesia)

Mice in Cream (Arctic)

Starling Stew with Olives (Turkey)

Stewed Cane Rat (Ghana)

Water-Beetle Cocktail Sauce (Laos)

Turtle Ragout (Mexico)

Stuffed Bear's Paw (Romania)

Red-Ant Chutney (India)

Baked Muskrat (Canada)

Raw Octopus (Hawaii)

Calf's Lung and Heart in a Paprika Sauce (Hungary)

Fox Tongues (Japan)

Pig's Face (Ireland)

Silkworm-Pupae Soup (Vietnam)

Cajun Squirrel Ravioli (United States)

Turtle Casserole (Fiji)

Lambs' Tails and Honey (Morocco)

Sun-Dried Maggots (China)

Pallbearers for Famous People

Phil Everly, for Buddy Holly

Ben Crenshaw, for Harvey Penick

Jack Lemmon, for Rosalind Russell

John McEnroe, for Vitas Gerulaitis

Emerson Fittipaldi, for Ayrton Senna

James Stewart, for Clark Gable

Hubert de Givenchy, for Audrey Hepburn

Tom Mix, for Wyatt Earp

Joe Louis, for Sonny Liston

King Edward VII, for William Gladstone

Kenny Rogers, for Vincente Minnelli

Rock Hudson, Frank Sinatra, Laurence Olivier, Gregory Peck, David Niven, Fred Astaire and Elia Kazan, for Natalie Wood

George Clooney, for Rosemary Clooney

Classic Songs That Stalled at Number 2—and What Beat Them to the Top

Number 2	Number 1
"Start Me Up" (The Rolling Stones)	**"Private Eyes"** (Hall & Oates)
"Proud Mary" (Creedence Clearwater Revival)	**"Dizzy"** (Tommy Roe)
"Bad Moon Rising" (Creedence Clearwater Revival)	***"Love Theme from Romeo & Juliet"*** (Henry Mancini & Orchestra)
"Dancing in the Street" (Martha & the Vandellas)	**"Do Wah Diddy Diddy"** (Manfred Mann)
"The Twist" (Chubby Checker)	**"Peppermint Twist—Part I"** (Joey Dee & the Starliters)
"Another Brick in the Wall" (Pink Floyd)	**"Call Me"** (Blondie)
"Return to Sender" (Elvis Presley)	**"Big Girls Don't Cry"** (The Four Seasons)
"Wild Thing" (The Troggs)	**"Hanky Panky"** (Tommy James & the Shondells)

"Light My Fire"
(The Doors)

"Be My Baby"
(The Ronettes)

"What's Going On"
(Marvin Gaye)

"Like a Rolling Stone"
(Bob Dylan)

"I'm Not in Love"
(10cc) City

"Daydream"
(The Lovin' Spoonful)

"Dancing in the Dark"
(Bruce Springsteen)

"Louie Louie"
(The Kingsmen)

"All You Need Is Love"
(The Beatles)

"Sugar Shack"
(Jimmy Gilmer & the
Fireballs)

"Joy to the World"
(Three Dog Night)

"Help!"
(The Beatles)

"The Hustle"
(Van McCoy & the
Soul Symphony)

**"(You're My) Soul and
Inspiration"** (The
Righteous Brothers)

"When Doves Cry"
(Prince)

"There! I've Said It Again"
(Bobby Vinton)

All the Breeds of Dog That Have Been "Best in Show" at Westminster

2005: German shorthaired pointer

2004: Newfoundland

2003: Kerry blue terrier

2002: Miniature poodle

2001: Bichon frisé

2000: English springer spaniel

1999: Papillon

1998: Norwich terrier

1997: Standard schnauzer

1996: Clumber spaniel

1995: Scottish terrier

1994: Norwich terrier

1993: English springer spaniel

1992: Wire fox terrier

1991: Standard poodle

1990: Pekingese

1989: Doberman pinscher

1988: Pomeranian

1987: German shepherd

1986: Pointer

1985: Scottish terrier

1984: Newfoundland

1983: Afghan hound

1982: Pekingese

1981: Pug

1980: Siberian husky

1979: Irish water spaniel

1978: Yorkshire terrier

1977: Sealyham terrier

1976: Lakeland terrier

1975: Old English sheepdog

1974: German shorthaired pointer

1973: Standard poodle

1972: English springer spaniel

1971: English springer spaniel

1970: Boxer

1969: Skyeterrier

1968: Lakeland terrier

1967: Scottish terrier

1966: Wire fox terrier

1965: Scottish terrier

1964: Whippet

1963: English springer spaniel

1962: West Highland white terrier

1961: Toy poodle

1960: Pekingese

1959: Miniature poodle

1958: Standard poodle

1957: Afghan hound

1956: Toy poodle

1955: Bulldog

1954: Cocker spaniel

1953: Doberman pinscher

1952: Doberman pinscher

1951: Boxer

1950: Scottish terrier

1949: Boxer

1948: Bedlington terrier

1947: Boxer

1946: Wire fox terrier

1945: Scottish terrier

1944: Welsh terrier

1943: Miniature poodle

1942: West Highland white terrier

1941: Cocker spaniel

1940: Cocker spaniel

1939: Doberman pinscher

1938: English setter

1937: Wire fox terrier

1936: Sealyham terrier

1935: Standard poodle

1934: Wire fox terrier

1933: Airedale terrier

1932: Pointer

1931: Wire fox terrier

1930: Wire fox terrier

1929: Collie

1928: Wire fox terrier

1927: Sealyham terrier

1926: Wire fox terrier

1925: Pointer

1924: Sealyham terrier

1923: There was no "Best in Show" title awarded

1922: Airedale terrier

1921: Cocker spaniel

1920: Wire fox terrier

1919: Airedale terrier

1918: Bull terrier

1917: Wire fox terrier

1916: Wire fox terrier

1915: Wire fox terrier

1914: Old English sheepdog

1913: Bulldog

1912: Airedale terrier

1911: Scottish terrier

1910: Smooth fox terrier

1909: Smooth fox terrier

1908: Smooth fox terrier

1907: Smooth fox terrier

Statistically the Most Landed-Upon Monopoly Squares

In order:

Illinois Avenue

Go

B&O Railroad

Free Parking

Tennessee Avenue

New York Avenue

Reading Railroad

St. James Place

Water Works

Pennsylvania Railroad

The 20 Most Popular States to Retire To

Florida

California

Arizona

Texas

North Carolina

Pennsylvania

New Jersey (no kidding—
the shore)

Washington

Virginia

Georgia

Ohio

Oregon

Nevada

New York

Illinois

Tennessee

Missouri

South Carolina

Maryland

Michigan

The 20 States That Lose the Most Retirees to Other States

New York

California

Florida (they tend to move to North Carolina)

Illinois

New Jersey

Pennsylvania

Michigan

Ohio

Texas

Massachusetts

Virginia

Connecticut

Maryland

Indiana

Arizona

Missouri

Wisconsin

Washington

Colorado

Georgia

The 20 Cities That Receive the Most Retirees

Phoenix, Arizona

West Palm/Boca Raton, Florida

Fort Lauderdale, Florida

St. Petersburg, Florida

Las Vegas, Nevada

Fort Myers, Florida

Los Angeles, California

Sarasota, Florida

New Port Richey, Florida

Miami, Florida

San Diego, Florida

Tucson, Arizona

Daytona Beach, Florida

Winter Haven, Florida

Melbourne, Florida

Naples, Florida

Tampa, Florida

Palm Springs, California

Port Charlotte, Florida

Bradenton, Florida

The Winning Word in All the National Spelling Bees

1925: gladiolus

1926: abrogate

1927: luxuriance

1928: albumen

1929: asceticism

1930: fracas

1931: foulard

1932: knack

1933: propitiatory

1934: deteriorating

1935: intelligible

1936: interning

1937: promiscuous

1938: sanitarium

1939: canonical

1940: therapy

1941: initials

1942: sacrilegious

1943–45: NO SPELLING
BEE WAS HELD

1946: semaphore

1947: chlorophyll

1948: psychiatry

1949: dulcimer

1950: haruspex

1951: insouciant

1952: vignette

1953: soubrette

1954: transept

1955: crustaceology

1956: condominium

1957: schappe

1958: syllepsis

1959: cacolet

1960: troche

1961: smaragdine

1962: esquamulose

1963: equipage

1964: sycophant

1962: esquamulose

1965: eczema

1966: ratoon

1967: chihuahua

1968: abalone

1969: interlocutory

1970: croissant

1971: shalloon

1972: macerate

1973: vouchsafe

1974: hydrophyte

1975: incisor

1976: narcolepsy

1977: cambist

1978: deification

1979: maculature

1980: elucubrate

1981: sarcophagus

1982: psoriasis

1983: purim

1984: luge

1985: milieu

1986: odontalgia

1987: staphylococci

1988: elegiacal

1989: spoliator

1990: fibranne

1991: antipyretic

1992: lyceum

1993: kamikaze

1994: antediluvian

1995: xanthosis

1996: vivisepulture

1997: euonym

1998: chiaroscurist

1999: logorrhea

2000: demarche

2001: succedaneum

2002: prospicience

2003: pococurante

2004: autochthonous

2005: appoggiatura

The International Ice Cream Association's Most Popular Flavors

Vanilla

Chocolate

Neapolitan

Nut (includes: almond, butter
pecan, pecan and other nuts)

Butter Pecan

Candy

Chocolate Chip

Mint Chocolate Chip

Cake/Cookies/Brownies

Coffee

All the Doublespeak Awards

(Presented by the Committee on Public Doublespeak, of the National Council of Teachers of English)

2005: Philip A. Cooney, Chief of Staff for the White House Council on Environmental Quality (for his ability to massage the language in his scientific reports to deflect the public's attention from the truth)

2004: The Bush Admistration (President George W. Bush, for the second year in a row, has set a high standard for his team by the inspired inventing of the term "weapons of mass destruction—related program activities" to describe what has yet to be seen . . .)

2003: President George W. Bush (for his creative use of language in public statements regarding the reasons the United States needed to pursue war against Iraq)

2002: New York State Board of Regents (for its "politically correct" and silent editing of state tests)

2001: Department of Defense (for creatively reporting the Missile Defense Systems test failure as "every flight is a success")

2000: The tobacco industry (for its media blitzes portraying tobacco companies as the benefactors of children, abused women and disaster victims— "abusing language in pursuit of their right to sell a deadly drug")

1999: National Rifle Association (excerpts were provided from two speeches to show the NRA's "artful twisting of language to blur issues, the invocation of patriotism, reverence, love of freedom, and the opposing use of dread words to color the opposition")

1998: Supreme Court Justice Clarence Thomas (for using hypocritical, loaded and inexact language to mislead the public about his real nature and intentions)

1997: President Bill Clinton, Trent Lott and Newt Gingrich (for obfuscating language in the balanced-budget agreement)

1996: Joe Klein, *Primary Colors* (for concealing his authorship)

1995: Newt Gingrich (for the euphemisms and omissions in the Republican "Contract with America")

1994: Rush Limbaugh (for his grossly deceptive language as a broadcaster)

1993: Department of Defense (based on the General Accounting Office report about the DOD's misrepresentations to mislead Congress)

1992: President George Bush (for his language related to the Gulf War, education and taxes)

1991: Department of Defense (for obfuscation, jargon and euphemisms during the first Gulf War)

1990: President George Bush (on wetlands, the Panama invasion, Tiananmen Square and "no new taxes")

1989: The Exxon Corporation (for the "Exxon Valdez" oil spill obfuscation)

1988: Secretary of Defense Frank Carlucci (for his comments about the downing of Iran Air Flight 655 by the USS *Vincennes*)

1987: Lieutenant Colonel Oliver North (about the obfuscation and cover-up of the Iran-Contra affair)

1986: NASA (for its response to the space shuttle *Challenger* explosion)

1985: CIA (for the Psychological Warfare Manual prepared for the Nicaraguan war)

1984: U.S. State Department (for its euphemisms in its human rights reports, and Grenada invasion)

1983: President Ronald Reagan (for the "Peacekeeper" missile, and Nicaraguan statements)

1982: Republican National Committee (for inaccurately crediting Reagan with Social Security reforms)

1981: Alexander Haig, secretary of state (for obfuscation of the murder of three American nuns in El Salvador)

1980: President-Elect Ronald Reagan (for gross misrepresentations of his record during the campaign)

1979: The nuclear-power industry (for its euphemisms and jargon during the Three Mile Island accident)

1978: Earl Clinton Bolton (for a CIA memo suggesting ways to use language to conceal and obfuscate)

1977: The Pentagon and the Energy Department (for language cover-up of the neutron-bomb development)

1976: Yasser Arafat, PLO leader (for seemingly contradictory language about Israel)

1975: Colonel David Opfer, USAF press officer in Cambodia (for saying to reporters, after a raid, "You always write it's bombing, bombing, bombing. It's not bombing! It's air support!"

Geography

Tasmania has the cleanest air in the inhabited world.

The farthest point from any ocean would be in China.

There are no public toilets in Peru.

The Coca-Cola Company is the largest consumer of vanilla in the world.

Everything weighs 1 percent less at the equator.

More redheads are born in Scotland than in any other part of the world.

More Dumb Things People Have Said

"Everything that can be invented has been invented." (Charles H. Duell, Commissioner, U.S. Office of Patents, 1899)

"This 'telephone' has too many shortcomings to be seriously considered as a means of communication. The device is inherently of no value to us." (Western Union internal memo, 1876)

"Who the hell wants to hear actors talk?" (Harry Warner of Warner Brothers, 1927)

"My imagination refuses to see any sort of submarine doing anything but suffocating its crew." (H. G. Wells)

"The abdomen, the chest, and the brain will forever be shut from the intrusion of the wise and humane surgeon." (Sir John Ericksen, Queen Victoria's surgeon, 1873)

"Louis Pasteur's theory of germs is ridiculous fiction." (Pierre Pachet, professor of physiology, 1872)

"No flying machine will ever fly from New York to Paris." (Orville Wright)

"Drill for oil? You mean drill into the ground to try and find oil? You're crazy." (Drillers responding to Edwin L. Drake in 1859 when he tried to persuade them to drill for oil)

"If we can just get young people to do as their fathers did, that is wear condoms." (Richard Branson)

"The wireless music box has no imaginable commercial value. Who would pay for a message sent to nobody in particular?" (Anonymous businessman declining to invest in radio in the 1920s)

"So we went to Atari and said, 'Hey, we've got this amazing thing, even built with some of your parts, and what do you think about funding us? Or we'll give it to you. We just want to do it. Pay our salary, we'll come work for you.' And they said, 'No.' So then we went to Hewlett-Packard, and they said, 'Hey, we don't need you. You haven't got through college yet.'" (Apple Computer cofounder Steve Jobs)

"Airplanes are interesting toys but of no military value."
(Marshal Foch)

"I'm just glad it'll be Clark Gable who's falling on his face
and not Gary Cooper." (Gary Cooper turning down the
role of Rhett Butler in *Gone With the Wind*)

"Heavier-than-air flying machines are impossible."
(Lord Kelvin, president of the Royal Society
talking in 1895)

"Stocks have reached what
looks like a permanently
high plateau." (Irving Fisher,
professor of economics at
Yale just before the 1929
Wall Street crash)

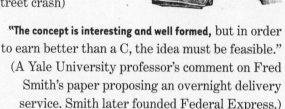

"The concept is interesting and well formed, but in order
to earn better than a C, the idea must be feasible."
(A Yale University professor's comment on Fred
Smith's paper proposing an overnight delivery
service. Smith later founded Federal Express.)

Slogans Seen Outside Churches

"No God—no peace. Know God—know peace."

"Free trip to heaven. Details inside!"

"Try our Sundays. They're better than Baskin-Robbins."

"**Have trouble sleeping?** We have sermons—come hear one!"

"**God so loved the world** that He did not send a committee."

"**When down in the mouth,** remember Jonah. He came out all right."

"**Sign broken.** Message inside this Sunday."

"**How will you spend eternity**—smoking or nonsmoking?"

"**Dusty Bibles lead** to dirty lives."

"**Come work for the Lord.** The work is hard, the hours are long, and the pay is low. But the retirement benefits are out of this world."

"**It is unlikely** there'll be a reduction in the wages of sin."

"**Do not wait for the** hearse to take you to church."

"**If you're headed** in the wrong direction, God allows U-turns."

"**Forbidden fruit creates** many jams."

"**In the dark?** Follow the Son."

"**If you can't sleep,** don't count sheep. Talk to the Shepherd."

Quotes About Lawyers

"The first thing we do, let's kill all the lawyers." (William Shakespeare, *King Henry VI, Part II*)

"Ninety-nine percent of lawyers give the rest a bad name." (Steven Wright)

"A town that can't support one lawyer can always support two." (Lyndon B. Johnson)

"Woodpeckers and lawyers have long bills." (Dr. K. C. Allen)

"There is never a deed so foul that something couldn't be said for the guy. That's why there are lawyers." (Melvin Belli)

"I don't think you can make a lawyer honest by an act of legislature. You've got to work on his conscience. And his lack of conscience is what makes him a lawyer." (Will Rogers)

"The trouble with law is lawyers." (Clarence Darrow)

"Lawyers, I suppose, were children once." (Charles Lamb)

"To some lawyers all facts are created equal." (Felix Frankfurter)

"Between grand theft and a legal fee, there only stands a law degree." (Anonymous)

"[Lawyers are] people whose profession it is to disguise matters." (Sir Thomas More)

"If law school is so hard to get through, how come there are so many lawyers?" (Calvin Trillin)

"If you laid all of the lawyers in the world, end to end, on the equator—it would be a good idea to just leave them there." (Anonymous)

"God works wonders now and then. Behold! a Lawyer, an honest man." (Benjamin Franklin)

"Two farmer were arguing over the ownership of a cow. While one farmer pulled the head, the other pulled the tail. The lawyer sat in the middle milking the cow." (Hebrew proverb)

"The legal trade is nothing but a high-class racket." (Professor Fred Rodell)

"A lawyer is a learned gentleman who rescues your estate from your enemies and keeps it for himself." (Lord Brougham)

"It is the trade of lawyers to question everything, yield nothing, and to talk by the hour." (Thomas Jefferson)

"He saw a lawyer killing a viper on a dunghill hard by his own stable / And the Devil smiled, for it put him in mind of Cain and his brother Abel." (Samuel T. Coleridge)

"Lawyers are the only persons in whom ignorance of the law is not punished." (Jeremy Bentham)

"Old lawyers never die, they just lose their appeal." (Anonymous)

"What happens when a lawyer takes Viagra? He gets taller." (Anonymous)

"An incompetent attorney can delay a trial for months or years. A competent attorney can delay one even longer." (Evelle J. Younger)

"Lawyers are like rhinoceroses: thick-skinned, shortsighted, but always ready to charge." (Anonymous)

"Everyone ought to take every opportunity to blast lawyers." (Marlin Fitzwater)

"As we watched Judge Clarence Thomas's Supreme Court confirmation hearings, all of the commentators said the same thing: 'One of these people in the room is lying.' Do you believe that? You've got two lawyers and fourteen senators in the room, and only *one* of them is lying?" (Jay Leno)

"Lawyers spend a great deal of their time shoveling smoke." (Oliver Wendell Holmes)

"Win your lawsuit, lose your money." (Spanish proverb)

"**If all the lawyers were** hanged tomorrow, and their bones sold to a mah jong factory, we'd be freer and safer, and our taxes would be reduced by almost half." (H. L. Mencken)

"**A man may as well open an** oyster without a knife as a lawyer's mouth without a fee." (Barten Holyday)

"**A lawyer is a man who** helps you get what's coming to him." (Laurence J. Peter)

"**No poet ever interpreted nature** as freely as a lawyer interprets truth." (Jean Giraudoux)

"**[Lawyers are] those who** use the law as shoemakers use leather: rubbing it, pressing it, and stretching it with their teeth, all to the end of making it fit their purposes." (King Louis XII)

"**If it weren't for lawyers,** we wouldn't need them." (Anonymous)

"**How do you get along at** the office? Do you trust each other? Or does each have a separate safe for his money?" (Groucho Marx to his lawyer)

"**I think we may class the** lawyer in the natural history of monsters." (John Keats)

"**He is no lawyer who** cannot take two sides." (Charles Lamb)

Some Famous Women's Last Words

"Hold the cross high so I may see it through the flames!" (Joan of Arc, 1431)

"All my possessions for a moment of time." (Queen Elizabeth I, 1603)

"Excuse me, sir." (Marie Antoinette, queen of France, 1793, as she stepped on the executioner's foot)

"Nothing but death." (Jane Austen, when asked if she wanted anything, 1817)

"I lingered around them, under that benign sky; watched the moths fluttering among the heath and harebells; listened to the soft wind breathing through the grass; and wondered how anyone could ever imagine unquiet slumbers for the sleepers in that quiet earth." (Emily Brontë, 1848)

"Oh, I am not going to die, am I? He will not separate us, we have been so happy." (Charlotte Brontë, 1855, to her husband of nine months)

"Beautiful." (Elizabeth Barrett Browning, 1861, in answer to her husband's query as to how she was feeling)

"I must go in, the fog is rising." (Emily Dickinson, 1886)

"Is it not meningitis?" (Louisa May Alcott, 1888)

"It is unbelievable." (Mata Hari, 1917)

"Farewell, my friends. I go to glory." (Isadora Duncan, 1927)

"Get my swan costume ready." (Anna Pavlova, 1931)

"KHAQQ calling Itasca. We must be on you, but cannot see you. Gas is running low." (Amelia Earhart, 1937)

"What is the question?" (Gertrude Stein, 1946, after her lover, Alice B. Toklas, asked her, "What is the answer?")

"Is everybody happy? I want everybody to be happy. I know I'm happy." (Ethel Barrymore, 1959)

"Am I dying or is this my birthday?" (Lady Nancy Astor, 1964)

"Codeine . . . bourbon." (Tallulah Bankhead, 1968)

"Damn it! Don't you dare ask God to help me." (Joan Crawford, 1977, to her housekeeper, who was praying for her)

"My God. What's happened?" (Diana, Princess of Wales, 1997)

Acknowledgments

For the past twenty years, I've been collecting weird and wonderful facts, which I've been storing on bits of paper and, more recently, on my computer. Every few years I'll use some of it in a book or a newspaper series, but it's always been my ambition to be able to put together the most fascinating, extraordinary facts I had—or could find—in one volume. A sort of director's cut, if you like, of my whole career. The difficult part was not what to put in but what to take out.

Consequently, most of what you will read has been acquired organically. However, I would also like to acknowledge material culled from the Internet: particularly Proof That Hell Is Exothermic and The World's Greatest Urban Myth. I have tried to source these wonderful items, but to no avail. However, I'm sure that their original authors would appreciate this wider audience.

Meanwhile, I am continuing to mine the seams of trivia—in the fervent hope that *That Book* will become an annual publication. To that end, if you have any interesting facts (along the lines of the ones in this book) or come across something you think might work in a future edition, please send them to me at: thatbook@mail.com.

This book—or, rather, *That Book*—couldn't have seen the light of day without the extraordinary foresight, imagination and diligence of (in alphabetical order): Hugh Adams,

Luigi Bonomi, Penny Chorlton, Patrick Janson-Smith, Mari Roberts and Doug Young. I would like to thank the following people for their help, contributions and/or support (moral or otherwise): Russell Ash, Paul Ashford, Jeremy Beadle, Marcus Berkmann, Paul Donnelley, Steve Elson, Chris Ewins, Jonathan Fingerhut, Alan Fox, Jenny Garrison, Cesar Garza, Brian Johnson, Andy Kay, John Koski, Richard Littlejohn, Tricia Martin, Emanuel Mond, William Mulcahy, Rex Newman, Nicholas Ridge, David Roth-Ey, Chris Tarrant, David Thomas, Roy Wells and Rob Woolley.

I would also like to take this opportunity to pay tribute to David Wallechinsky. It was the pioneering work done by him and his family on the seminal Books of Lists that originally excited my interest in this sort of work.

If I've missed anyone, then please know that—as with any mistakes in the book—it's entirely down to my own stupidity: forgive me.

List of Lists

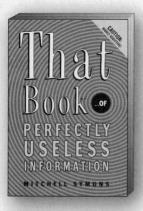

THAT BOOK
. . . of Perfectly
Useless Information
ISBN 0-06-073254-7 (paperback)

The ultimate trivia guide. Organized in
thematic sections, *That Book* covers a world
of learning. Want to know which U.S.
president is a descendant of King Edward
III? Or which famous people lived to read
their own obituaries? *That Book* covers these
inessential facts and more . . .

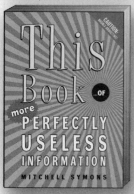

THIS BOOK
. . . of More Perfectly
Useless Information
ISBN 0-06-082824-2 (paperback)

Another treasure trove of extraordinary facts
and mind-boggling trivia. Whether you're
trying to show off in front of your coworkers
around the water cooler or hoping to impress
a member of the opposite sex, *This Book . . .
Of More Perfectly Useless Information* is for you.

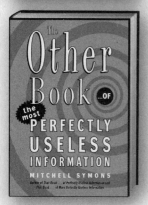

THE OTHER BOOK
. . . of the Most Perfectly
Useless Information
ISBN 0-06-113405-8 (hardcover)

The third book in Mitchell Symons' trivia
trifecta, *The Other Book* is chock full of
scientific facts, sporting stats, celebrity gossip,
and much, much more.